Democracy

Other Books in the History of Issues Series

THE HISTORY OF ISSUES

Democracy

Uma Kukathas, Book Editor

GREENHAVEN PRESS
A part of Gale, Cengage Learning

GALE
CENGAGE Learning

Detroit • New York • San Francisco • New Haven, Conn • Waterville, Maine • London

Christine Nasso, *Publisher*
Elizabeth Des Chenes, *Managing Editor*

© 2008 Greenhaven Press, a part of Gale, Cengage Learning

Gale and Greenhaven Press are registered trademarks used herein under license.

For more information, contact:
Greenhaven Press
27500 Drake Rd.
Farmington Hills, MI 48331-3535
Or you can visit our Internet site at gale.cengage.com

For product information and technology assistance, contact us at

Gale Customer Support, 1-800-877-4253
For permission to use material from this text or product, submit all requests online at www.cengage.com/permissions

Further permissions questions can be emailed to permissionrequest@cengage.com

Articles in Greenhaven Press anthologies are often edited for length to meet page require-ments. In addition, original titles of these works are changed to clearly present the main thesis and to explicitly indicate the author's opinion. Every effort is made to ensure that Greenhaven Press accurately reflects the original intent of the authors. Every effort has been made to trace the owners of copyrighted material.

Cover image copyright David H. Seymour, 2008. Used under license from Shutterstock.com.

LIBRARY OF CONGRESS CATALOGING-IN-PUBLICATION DATA

Democracy / Uma Kukathas, book editor.
    p. cm. -- (History of issues)
    Includes bibliographical references and index.
    ISBN 978-0-7377-3971-8 (hardcover)
    1. Democracy. I. Kukathas, Uma.
    JC423.D44144 2008
    321.8--dc22

                                                                2008010048

Printed in the United States of America
1 2 3 4 5 6 7 12 11 10 09 08

Contents

Chapter 3: Modern Democracy Beyond the West

Foreword

In the 1940s, at the height of the Holocaust, Jews struggled to create a nation of their own in Palestine, a region of the Middle East that at the time was controlled by Britain. The British had placed limits on Jewish immigration to Palestine, hampering efforts to provide refuge to Jews fleeing the Holocaust. In response to this and other British policies, an underground Jewish resistance group called Irgun began carrying out terrorist attacks against British targets in Palestine, including immigration, intelligence, and police offices. Most famously, the group bombed the King David Hotel in Jerusalem, the site of a British military headquarters. Although the British were warned well in advance of the attack, they failed to evacuate the building. As a result, ninety-one people were killed (including fifteen Jews) and forty-five were injured.

Early in the twentieth century, Ireland, which had long been under British rule, was split into two countries. The south, populated mostly by Catholics, eventually achieved independence and became the Republic of Ireland. Northern Ireland, mostly Protestant, remained under British control. Catholics in both the north and south opposed British control of the north, and the Irish Republican Army (IRA) sought unification of Ireland as an independent nation. In 1969, the IRA split into two factions. A new radical wing, the Provisional IRA, was created and soon undertook numerous terrorist bombings and killings throughout Northern Ireland, the Republic of Ireland, and even in England. One of its most notorious attacks was the 1974 bombing of a Birmingham, England, bar that killed nineteen people.

In the mid-1990s, an Islamic terrorist group called al Qaeda began carrying out terrorist attacks against American targets overseas. In communications to the media, the organization listed several complaints against the United States. It generally opposed all U.S. involvement and presence in the Middle East. It particularly objected to the presence of U.S. troops in Saudi Arabia, which is the home of several Islamic holy sites. And it strongly condemned the United States for supporting the nation of Israel, which it claimed was an oppressor of Muslims. In 1998 al Qaeda's leaders issued a fatwa (a religious legal statement) calling for Muslims to kill Americans. Al Qaeda acted on this order many times—most memorably on September 11, 2001, when it attacked the World Trade Center and the Pentagon, killing nearly three thousand people.

These three groups—Irgun, the Provisional IRA, and al Qaeda—have achieved varied results. Irgun's terror campaign contributed to Britain's decision to pull out of Palestine and to support the creation of Israel in 1948. The Provisional IRA's tactics kept pressure on the British, but they also alienated many would-be supporters of independence for Northern Ireland. Al Qaeda's attacks provoked a strong U.S. military response but did not lessen America's involvement in the Middle East nor weaken its support of Israel. Despite these different results, the means and goals of these groups were similar. Although they emerged in different parts of the world during different eras and in support of different causes, all three had one thing in common: They all used clandestine violence to undermine a government they deemed oppressive or illegitimate.

The destruction of oppressive governments is not the only goal of terrorism. For example, terror is also used to minimize dissent in totalitarian regimes and to promote extreme ideologies. However, throughout history the motivations of terrorists have been remarkably similar, proving the old adage that "the more things change, the more they remain the same." Arguments for and against terrorism thus boil down to the same set of universal arguments regardless of the age: Some argue that terrorism is justified to change (or, in the case of state terror, to maintain) the prevailing political order; others respond that terrorism is inhumane and unacceptable under any circumstances. These basic views transcend time and place.

Similar fundamental arguments apply to other controversial social issues. For instance, arguments over the death penalty have always featured competing views of justice. Scholars cite biblical texts to claim that a person who takes a life must forfeit his or her life, while others cite religious doctrine to support their view that only God can take a human life. These arguments have remained essentially the same throughout the centuries. Likewise, the debate over euthanasia has persisted throughout the history of Western civilization. Supporters argue that it is compassionate to end the suffering of the dying by hastening their impending death; opponents insist that it is society's duty to make the dying as comfortable as possible as death takes its natural course.

Greenhaven Press's *The History of Issues* series illustrates this constancy of arguments surrounding major social issues. Each volume in the series focuses on one issue—including terrorism, the death penalty, and euthanasia—and examines how the debates have both evolved and remained essentially the same over the years. Primary documents such as newspaper articles, speeches, and government reports illuminate historical developments and offer perspectives from throughout history. Secondary sources provide overviews and commentaries from a more contemporary perspective. An introduction begins each anthology and supplies essential context and background. An annotated table of contents, chronology, and index allow for easy reference, and a bibliography and list of organizations to contact point to additional sources of information on the book's topic. With these features, *The History of Issues* series permits readers to glimpse both the historical and contemporary dimensions of humanity's most pressing and controversial social issues.

Introduction

In January 2005, in his inaugural address opening his second term in office, U.S. president George W. Bush pledged to continue his stated mission of spreading democracy around the world. "It is the policy of the United States," he announced, "to seek and support the growth of democratic movements and institutions in every nation and culture." These sentiments had been expressed beginning in Bush's first term, and had become particularly marked after the events of September 11, 2001. In speeches at home and abroad, the president argued that the only way to guarantee the freedom of the United States was to ensure that other countries adopt its political principles. Declaring democracy an "antidote to radicalism and terror," he insisted too that the war in Iraq would bring democracy and peace to the Middle East.

For Bush, democracy has been offered up as an unquestionably worthy social and political goal, a hallowed ideal whose promotion around the world is totally justified. He holds the view, like many Westerners, that democracy is the best form of government, and one that all people want—or should want. Bush has asserted often that oppressed peoples "crave democracy" and that only a world based on democratic principles can be peaceful. He has also repeatedly equated democracy with freedom, understanding the two to be essentially synonymous. However, Bush's desire to promote democracy has been heavily criticized, both at home and abroad. His detractors say that, given that the nation has been engaged in an unpopular war since 2003 and the popularity of the United States in the rest of the world is at an all-time low, the effectiveness of pushing American policies to hasten democratization are questionable at best. Others have rejected the idea that democracy, no matter the shape it takes, is the answer to the world's ills.

Yet even among Bush's opponents, there is a strong belief that democracy is indeed an ideal to which all nations should aspire. Some of his harshest critics agree that democracy is an essential good for human beings. Around the world, popular protests have shown that many people want democracy. In 2007, several countries, notably Myanmar, formerly Burma, and Cambodia, saw mass demonstrations calling for democratic reforms. Indeed, in a poll taken by Worldopinion.org, it was found that most people around the world share Bush's belief that democracy is the most favorable form of government. Majorities in 66 out of 67 countries agreed that "democracy may have its problems but it is still better than any other form of government."

Why, then, do Bush's critics reject his idea that the United States has an obligation to "spread democracy" around the world? The main reason, as also reported by Worldopinion.org, is that there is widespread belief that the policies of the Bush administration do not show a respect for democratic principles even as it purports to impart them to the rest of the world. According to many of Bush's opponents, the president's notion of democracy is not true democracy at all. The question, then, is what does Bush mean when he talks of "democracy"? And what do others mean by it? And how can there be such disparity regarding something that is almost universally regarded as a good thing?

Defining Democracy

Political philosophers have pointed out for hundreds of years that "democracy" is a much-abused term. The philosopher John Austin remarked that democracy is a "useless word," and contemporary political scientists generally prefer not to use it because it is both vague and loaded. Today, news reports often use the word to define American and Western European culture and values and point out the shortcomings of those with different systems of government. However, dictators have also invoked it to insist that freedoms must be curbed in the service of the people. Even school reformers mention it when lamenting the poor state of education today. Democracy is different things to different people, but is almost always used, says the historian Roland N. Stromberg in *Democracy: A Short Analytic History*, as a "hurrah word." To say that something is democratic is often to imply that it is right, good, and true. Politicians rally around the term to show that they are correct and true; their policies should be adopted, they imply, because not to do so would be undemocratic and therefore unacceptable.

There is a great deal of controversy as to what the term even means, however, and the history of democracy as a political system is long and varied. "Democracy" literally means "rule of the people," from the Greek "demos" ("people") and "kratos" (rule or power). Webster's dictionary defines it as "government in which the supreme power is vested in the people and exercised by them directly or indirectly through a system of representation usually involving periodically held free elections." Abraham Lincoln called it government "of the people, by the people, for the people." However, democracy is more than majority rule, or a government in which the people elect their representatives (which is the definition of a republic).

To further complicate things, there are different types of democracies. In a direct democracy, individuals participate directly in making laws and decisions. By contrast, in a representative democracy, citizens elect officials to represent their interests in government decisions. An anarchist democracy is an example of a direct democracy, while socialist and liberal democracies are representative democracies. The democracy practiced in the United States is liberal democracy (or constitutional democracy), which involves separation of the state's powers, recognition of basic rights, religious liberty, and separation of church and state. In this form of government, a constitution guarantees basic personal and political rights, fair and free elections, and independent courts of law.

When American news reporters and politicians refer to "democracy," they usually mean liberal democracy, which is the form of democracy also found in Australia, Britain, New Zealand, Canada, and many western European nations. A liberal democracy is quite different from the democracy of a country like, for example, Singapore. Although Singapore is recognized as a representative democracy, the same political party has been in power since it became independent in 1959, despite having regular elections; the government also curbs what many view as the basic democratic right of free speech. Singapore is often criticized by Western governments for its "undemocratic practices," which in effect means that its practices do not conform to liberal democratic standards.

When Bush asserts that he wishes to bring democracy to the rest of the world, he has in mind Western liberal democracy, with its constitutional features and complement of rights. However, many leaders and citizens in the rest of the world disagree that this type of democracy should be upheld as the standard for the world to follow. They assert that this type of democracy is infused with Western cultural values that other countries should not be forced to adopt, including rights of free speech, freedom of religion, and controversial rights concerning sexuality. But many Westerners believe that in the twenty-first century, liberal democracy is the only just form of democracy. However, some argue as well that Bush's brand of democracy is not true liberal democracy at all.

The current disagreement and debate among these different supporters of democracy, then, lies in what they view as the basic principles of democracy. Each group champions democracy, but their understanding of it differs widely. A quick survey of the history of democracy shows why there are such widely converging beliefs.

The Origins of Democracy

While there is some evidence that democratic systems of government flourished in Asia and the Middle East as long ago as 2500 BCE, most historians hold that the earliest, or at least the most important, democracy began in Athens in the fifth century BCE The first democracy was a response to power being in the hands of a select group, which is the same reason democracy is championed today. The brutal dictator Hippias made life for Athenian citizens increasingly difficult, and the aristocrat Cleisthenes obtained help from the Spartans to overthrow him. After Hippias was deposed in 510 BCE, it looked like Cleisthenes could seize power. However, he was challenged by another nobleman, Isagoras, who appealed to the Spartans for support. Cleisthenes responded by appealing for supporters far beyond the normal factions of the aristocracy and proposing a radical political reform movement that in 508/507 BCE ushered in the Athenian democratic constitution.

A number of military victories under this system of rule bolstered Athenians' belief in democracy, and they began to dominate the region, becoming the leaders of nearly all Greece and exporting democracy throughout their empire. In the late 460s BCE Ephialtes and Pericles presided over a radicalization of power by bringing forward legislation that let anyone, regardless of birth or wealth, serve as a city leader or magistrate. Pericles, one of ten elected generals, soon enjoyed overwhelming support of the populace, and with his superlative oratory powers and charisma dominated the democratic government of Athens for thirty years. He also transformed the city-state into the cultural capital of the world, a center of arts and learning, and pushed through a series of reforms. His famous funeral oration for the fallen soldiers of the Peloponnesian War, as reported by the historian Thucydides, is regarded as one of the great statements of the value of participatory democracy and the form of government where "everyone is equal before the law."

The democracy of ancient Athens was unlike American democracy today. It was a direct democracy and, with a few exceptions, Athenians did not vote for politicians to represent them but rather voted on every law or policy the city was to adopt. Elected officials held more practical posts, for example as tax collectors and jurists. Not all Athenians were eligible to vote; that right was restricted to male citizens born in Athens and whose parents were also born in the city. Neither slaves nor foreigners nor women could vote. Thus only about 10 percent of the population of Athens at the time was eligible to participate in the "rule of the people." Importantly, only those with considerable leisure time would participate in a form of democracy that required as much direct involvement as Athenian democracy. This was made possible by the fact that even the poorest Athenian citizen could afford to have slaves to attend to his work while he busied himself with civic and political affairs. Further, it has been shown that because Athens depended so heavily on its navy, it was seen as prudent to allow skilled seamen to have political power—this class of relatively poor Athenians was huge in number, and the city depended on them for their security and thus it was necessary to give them political power if the city was to survive. However, Athenian democracy also promoted ideas that have become important features of contemporary liberal democratic government, including free speech, the election of officials, and constraints on the power of those holding office.

While Pericles was loved by many, he was criticized by his opponents as a demagogue who led his people into a catastrophic war. Some, including the historian Plutarch, have implied that his support was gained using less than scrupulous methods, including offering poor citizens festival grants and other wages to gain their support. Thucydides wrote that Athens was "in name a democracy, but in fact a government by the greatest citizen." Although Pericles championed the cause of a government in which the many and not the few controlled state affairs, he wielded extraordinary power. Democracy continued to thrive after Pericles's death in 429 BCE, but the war that he began with the Spartans two years earlier would eventually bring about the downfall of Athens. Although the city-state survived the war, and would continue for another eighty years, democracy was criticized by most of the influential thinkers of the time. The philosopher Plato, whose teacher Socrates was executed at the hands of the democratic people's court in 399 BCE for "corrupting the youth of Athens" with his ideas, viewed democracy as unjust and prone to abuse. His ideas were prescient, and by 338 BCE, the Athenian empire had withered and was conquered by Philip of Macedon, father of Alexander the Great.

Roman Republicanism

Although the Athenian empire had fallen, democracy did not completely die with it. The Romans adopted many of the principles of the Greeks in their system of government, and democracy flourished there for the next three hundred years. Democracy had originally appeared in the Italian city around the same time it did in Athens, and their system, which they called *respublica* ("republic"; "the thing that belongs to the people") lasted until roughly the end of the first century BCE Roman republicanism was a representative democracy, with delegates from the nobility in its Senate and representatives from the commoners in its Assembly. Governmental power was divided between the two branches, and they voted on various issues.

Many Roman political thinkers supported the ideals of democracy. The statesman Cicero advocated it and argued that all people have certain rights that should be preserved in a democratic state. However, he acknowledged too that democracy often degenerates into mob rule. The demise of the Roman republic, ironically, was due to the incredible power the city had gained after a series of wars. As Rome's economy shifted from one of labor by freedmen into that of slavery, a new aristocracy arose. Augustus Caesar, an elected general, soon seized power and retained it with the support of the new elite, becoming the first ruler of the new Roman Empire.

The Development of Modern Democracy

After Caesar installed himself as emperor in 27 BCE, democracy all but disappeared for more than a thousand years. In most of Europe, Africa, and Asia, people were governed in feudal systems or were under the rule of monarchs. In AD 1215, the Magna Carta opened the door to a more democratic system in England. King John was forced to sign this "Great Charter" that created the English parliament, stating that the written laws held a higher power than the king, thereby limiting the power of the monarchy and giving the people some authority. Centuries later, in 1689, the Bill of Rights granted freedom of speech and banned cruel punishment. While such reforms did not usher in democracy, they did give rise to a new way of thinking about governance.

It was during the Age of Enlightenment in Europe, from the late seventeenth century through the end of the eighteenth century, that the intellectual foundation of what is now known as modern constitutional democracy was laid. During this period rationalism was regarded as supreme, and many traditional social, religious, and political ideas were rejected.

The first important work espousing the principles of liberal democracy was *Two Treatises of Government* written in 1690 by the English philosopher John Locke. In his book Locke proposed the idea of "natural law" to refute the notion that monarchy was an aspect of a divinely ordained chain of being. Natural law, he argued, guarantees men their natural rights—to life, certain liberties, ownership of property, and the fruits of their own labor. To secure these rights, men in civil society enter into a "social contract" with their government. They choose their governments, and governments agree to uphold their obligations laid out in the contract. Citizens are bound to obey the law, while the government must protect citizens, making laws and defending them from foreign injury. Locke asserted that when government becomes lawless and arbitrary, citizens have the right to overthrow it and install a new one. Like the early Athenian democrats, Locke was responding to a system in which monarchs held complete power and the people were to a large extent bound by their whims. Natural law assured men that they had authority to govern themselves. In 1762 the French philosopher Jean-Jacques Rousseau expanded on Locke's idea in *The Social Contract*. Offering the radical view that ordinary people should have a say in how their government is run, Locke and Rousseau paved the way for American democracy.

Early American Democracy

Beginning in 1763, Britain began imposing taxes on its colonists in America. Having no representation in Britain, many colonists declared this taxation to be illegal. To suppress protests, Britain sent in troops, and in 1775 the Revolutionary War began. A year later, representatives of the thirteen colonies voted unanimously to declare their independence from Britain and form the United States of America. When Thomas Jefferson wrote the Declaration of Independence in 1776, he borrowed heavily from the ideas of both Locke and Rousseau. Jefferson echoed Locke's notions that all men are created equal, and claimed that people have what he called "inalienable" rights—which he declared to be life, liberty, and the pursuit of happiness. Jefferson borrowed Rousseau's idea that if the government does not recognize man's natural rights then citizens have the right to take up arms against it. The colonists did just that when they waged the Revolutionary War and declared themselves independent from Britain.

The U.S. Constitution, adopted eleven years later and made effective in 1789, sets out the basic mechanics and principles of how the American government should work. The document reflects that the new government was radically different from others of its day. The first principle of the representative, elective government was that its power came from the people. The Constitution begins, "We the people," emphasizing the sovereignty of the citizenry. It also stresses that in this limited constitutional republic individual rights are strongly protected. It also emphasizes federalism and a system of checks and balances, but does not mention the word "democracy." In fact in the Federalist Papers, written between 1787 and 1788 to outline the philosophy of the U.S. Constitution, James Madison warns against the dangers of a democracy, specifically because of the potential for the "tyranny of the majority." He and other framers of the Constitution equate democracy with direct democracy, which they reject. Rather, they emphasize representative democracy and the protection of individual rights despite majority rule.

Yet despite the important distinction between a Republican form of government and a democracy, in popular usage the United States was called a democracy, because of the participation of its citizens in government. (It is important to note, however, that not everyone in the United States had the right to vote and pursue their freedom and happiness. Native Americans, whose land had been occupied by settlers, were not eligible to vote. Neither were women or black slaves, whether free or not. Only propertied white males over the age of twenty-one could vote in the new republic. This constituted about 16 percent of the non-Indian population, and much less if one counts Native Americans as well. Thus in the new United States of America, the percentage of people participating in the democratic system was less than in the early democracy in Athens.) In *Democracy in America*, published in 1835, the French political thinker and historian Alexis de Tocqueville describes the success of American democracy as well as its potential dangers. De Tocqueville refers to the American system as a "democracy" while discussing specifically its features as a republican representative government.

The Spread of Democracy
in the Twentieth Century

The nineteenth and twentieth centuries witnessed democratic forms of government springing up all over the world, after revolutions took place against monarchies and dictatorships. Before the end of the nineteenth century, most Western European monarchies had adopted a constitution limiting royal authority and giving some power to the people. After World War I, democracy flourished briefly in Europe, only to be interrupted by the Second World War. After 1945, representative governments were again established in many countries, although Central and Eastern Europe remained under Communist rule. In Asia, Japan adopted a democratic constitution after the war, and many former European colonies in Africa and Asia chose democratic forms of government in the 1950s and '60s after struggling for and achieving independence. Countries in southern Europe in the 1970s and Central Europe in the late 1980s implemented democratic systems. According to Freedom House, there are now 120 countries around the world that can be described as democratic that have functionally democratic institutions. In 1970, there had been fewer than one-third of that number.

Not all of these democracies, however, practice the liberal democracy advocated by the United States and other Western nations and organizations. Freedom House says that some of these countries have "restrictive democratic practices." For Freedom House, a democracy is understood as necessarily practicing competitive elections, and such elections require certain basic rights, including freedom of speech, freedom of the press, and rule of law. Their conception of democracy is liberal democracy. A 2006 study done by the *Economist* ranking countries in terms of their level of democracy similarly uses principles of liberal democracy as their standard. In making their determinations, the *Economist* looked at electoral process and pluralism, civil liberties, the functioning of government, political participation, and political culture to determine the most and least democratic countries in the world. They stressed that the condition of having free and fair competitive elections, and satisfying related aspects of political freedom, was clearly the basic requirement of all definitions.

Some countries, such as Singapore, believe that not adhering to such political principles does not make them undemocratic, and its leaders argue that while they put economic progress ahead of human rights, the country is nonetheless a democracy. Critics charge that Singapore's lack of press freedom and the existence of an Internal Security Act that allows the government to arbitrarily arrest citizens and detain them without trial does indeed make the country undemocratic. Singapore, however, counters that it is a success story, boasting economic, political, and social stability unlike anywhere on earth despite curbing its citizens' civil and political rights.

Singaporean critics of liberal democracy argue that the freedoms the United States requires under its system have led the country into corruption, inequality, and cultural decay—features not found in life in Singapore. Singapore routinely outperforms the United States in terms of education, and the crime rate is one of the lowest in the world. Thus, they say, the "freedoms" that are so commonly associated with American democracy are not necessarily a benefit, if they are freedoms at all, but an unwanted side effect of a form of democracy that requires a commitment to civil liberties.

Whose Democracy?

Interestingly, although Singapore is ranked low in terms of its "democracy index" (it ranks 87th out of 167 in the *Economist* study) it is not a country targeted by the United States as one that requires intervention, and neither is it publicly criticized for its restrictions on individual freedoms. Singapore is a close ally of the United States, and a large trading partner, and the Bush administration has deemphasized the "human rights" aspect of relations with Singapore because of the sensitivity surrounding that issue. Bush has also tempered his criticism of the authoritarian regimes in Saudi Arabia and Pakistan because of strategic interests. This has led critics of Bush to argue that the president's advocacy of democracy around the world has less to do with an interest in promoting democracy than with political and economic pragmatism.

Bush has reserved most of his criticism of nondemocratic regimes for Iran, branding it "the world's leading state-sponsor of terror." Bush's opponents, such as Phyllis Bennis with the Institute for Policy Studies in Washington, D.C., agree that Iran has a repressive political system (it ranks 139th on the *Economist*'s scale) and have denounced its record on human rights abuses. But they point out too that Bush's interest in Iran may not be based merely on principle, but on profit and oil; that country has substantial oil resources and it is in the strategic interests of the United States to be able to control it. Indeed, many contend that Bush does not promote liberal democracy because his interests have little to do with the principles of democracy that are under attack. It is no surprise then that the country's enemies might view it as a form of tyranny in which American interests and corporate, capitalist values are foisted upon the rest of the world.

Still, Bush's critics often agree that promoting democracy is a good thing. Michael Mandelbaum, a professor of American foreign policy at Johns Hopkins does not dispute the idea that democracy is a good form of government that should be promoted. But he criticizes the Bush administration for its misguided attempts to establish democracy in the Middle East. Military interventions, he contends, rarely result in the establishment of democracy; instead, he says, it is a voluntary adoption of the free-market system that tends to predict a switch toward democracy. Fareed Zakaria, writing for *News-week*, similarly points out that Bush's aggressive promotion of democracy overseas has in fact soured the world on representative government, the more so because others view the United States as an aggressive bully whose actions in Iran and Iraq have pointed to a lack of respect for national sovereignty and individual freedoms. Ohio Democratic senator Dennis J. Kucinich has also criticized Bush heavily for impinging on the liberties of Americans through legislation such as the USA Patriot Act and wiretapping citizens in defiance of the Constitution.

Four times as many countries have embraced democracy in the last four decades than in the world's history, but despite its being seen as a valuable asset, democracy is a source of much contention. Some countries, like Singapore, believe firmly that they are a genuine democracy because they hold elections to let their citizens decide who will represent them— which is seen by some as the main criteria for a democracy. Various countries use democracy as a "hurrah word" to deflect criticism of their policies. During Bush's visit to China in 2005, Chinese president Hu Jintao emphasized China's democratic nature, despite the fact that the country is seen as having one of the worst records on human rights and free and fair elections. Bush's critics say that he too uses the term "democracy" recklessly, invoking it when he seeks to promote U.S. economic interests that have nothing to do with fair elections and civil liberties. But the history of democracy shows that the very idea of democracy is a difficult one. For the Athenians, democracy was intertwined with pragmatism, as well. Cleisthenes promoted democratic reforms because without the help of the citizens Athens would have been lost to him. The Founding Fathers of the United States warned against democracy and the tyranny of the majority while denying the vote to all but a small fraction of the populace. In the twenty-first century, democracy continues to be a difficult concept to sort out. It is equated with political freedom and with a just system of government, but as long as people disagree about what that might mean, a satisfying definition of democracy is likely to be out of reach.

CHAPTER 1

Democracy in the Ancient World

Chapter Preface

Where did democracy begin? Although there is some evidence that non-Western societies as much as twenty-five hundred years ago embraced democratic values, most Western historians see Greece as the birthplace of democracy. Athens was among the first recorded democracies and certainly the most important Western democracy in ancient times. The modern term "democracy" (from *demokratia*, literally "rule by the people") was coined by the Athenians. In 508 BCE, after the overthrow of the tyrant Hippias, the nobleman Cleisthenes introduced a number of changes to Athenian government giving authority to the people of the city-state. For the first time, all Athenian citizens enjoyed legal and political equality. They were free to choose their rulers and to vote in public assemblies on important issues.

For more than a century and a half, Athens enjoyed a system of government that allowed it to expand territorially and lift Greek civilization to new heights. Under the rule of the politician-general Pericles, the court systems were completed and a jury system put into place. According to Pericles, Athens flourished during this time because of democracy. In Pericles's famous speech honoring the dead of the Peloponnesian War, he declared that Athens was supreme because its system of government allowed men to advance because of merit instead of wealth or class. In a democracy, he said, citizens behave lawfully while doing what they like without fear of prying eyes. And also, democracy ensures equal justice for all.

Pericles's sentiments closely resemble the official attitude of modern nations that favor democracy. Modern democracies certainly share many of the ideas and ideals of Athenian democracy, and can be said to have grown from the roots of the radical Greek experiment in governance. However, there are important differences between democracy as practiced in the ancient world and that found in the contemporary world. Ancient Greek democracy was "direct democracy," sometimes called "pure democracy." Constitutional power rested in the hands of citizens, and ideas were expressed directly through the Assembly, which consisted of all male citizens willing to attend sessions held several times a month. Citizens took their duties of participation seriously, and for good reason: Whatever the Assembly decided by vote was the law of the land.

This system is a clear contrast to most modern democracies, which are representative democracies, where sovereignty is exercised by a subset of the people, usually on the basis of election. In the United States, representatives chosen by the electorate form an independent ruling body that is responsible for acting in the people's interest. In U.S. national elections, the final decision of who will be president is in the hands of a separate voting body called the Electoral College. In the aftermath of the 2000 election between George W. Bush and Al Gore, much of the world was shocked that Bush was named winner, since Gore had more votes. Gore claimed the popular vote, but Bush, having won the Electoral College, was declared the next president. This seemed to many people to be simply "undemocratic"; how could it be that the country's ruler was not the choice of the majority of people?

The United States was conceived of by its founders as a republic, governed by representatives and not directly by citizens. The rationale for this is that the public is not in a position to best judge the appropriate actions of government. They thus need informed representatives who have more than a superficial understanding of politics and do not choose officials based on their charisma and what seems to be of personal benefit. Without such representation, there would be the danger of the "tyranny of the majority."

Interestingly, ancient writers pointing out the hazards of democracy warned against just these deficiencies, arguing that they would be the downfall of democracy. Plato, in the *Repub-*

lic, points out that the democratic man does not discern between what is desirable and what is good, and Marcus Tullius Cicero in his *On the Commonwealth* says that in democracy there is no distinction between citizens and thus democracy turns easily into mob rule. It might be said, then, that the Founding Fathers learned from the successes and errors of democracy's first practitioners, hearing the voices of its supporters as well as its critics. In establishing a representative democracy, they sought to uphold Pericles's vision of a system in which equal justice flourishes, but not at the expense of principle and good judgment.

The Ideals of Democracy

Thucydides

In The Peloponnesian Wars, *the former general Thucydides (ca. 460/455–ca. 399 BCE) provides an account of the war between Sparta and Athens. One of the most famous passages from Thucydides's history is the speech of the warrior-statesman Pericles, in which he offers his eloquent statement of the value of democracy. Asked to give the official funeral oration for the Athenian soldiers who had died at one of the opening battles, Pericles took the occasion not only to praise the dead, but Athens itself. In the address he speaks of the ideals of democracy, asserting that democracy allows men to advance because of merit instead of wealth or inherited class. He praises his city's freedom and says that in a democracy, citizens behave lawfully while doing what they like without fear of reprisal, and there is equal justice for all in private disputes. The speech has been viewed as enshrining the principles of democracy as well as offering justification for Athens's warlike and imperialist ambitions. It is unlikely that Pericles spoke exactly these words, since it was customary for ancient historians to invent the speeches of the figures they wrote about, but they do reflect what scholars regard as his views on democracy.*

In the same winter the Athenians, following their annual custom, gave a public funeral for those who had been the first to die in the war. These funerals are held in the following way: two days before the ceremony the bones of the fallen are brought and put in a tent which has been erected, and people make whatever offerings they wish to their own dead. Then there is a funeral procession in which coffins of cypress wood

Thucydides, "Pericles's Funeral Oration" (Book II), *History of the Peloponnesian War*, translated by Rex Warner, New York: Penguin Classics, 1954, revised edition 1972, pp. 34–46. Translation copyright © Rex Warner, 1954. Introduction and Appendices copyright © M. I. Finley, 1972. Used by permission of Penguin Books Ltd.

are carried on wagons. There is one coffin for each tribe, which contains the bones of members of that tribe. One empty bier is decorated and carried in the procession: this is for the missing, whose bodies could not be recovered. Everyone who wishes to, both citizens and foreigners, can join in the procession, and the women who are related to the dead are there to make their laments at the tomb. The bones are laid in the public burial-place, which is in the most beautiful quarter outside the city walls. Here the Athenians always bury those who have fallen in war. The only exception is those who died at Marathon, who, because their achievement was considered absolutely outstanding, were buried on the battlefield itself.

When the bones have been laid in the earth, a man chosen by the city for his intellectual gifts and for his general reputation makes an appropriate speech in praise of the dead, and after the speech all depart. This is the procedure at these burials, and all through the war, when the time came to do so, the Athenians followed this ancient custom. Now, at the burial of those who were the first to fall in the war Pericles, the son of Xanthippus, was chosen to make the speech. When the moment arrived, he came forward from the tomb and, standing on a high platform, so that he might be heard by as many people as possible in the crowd, he spoke as follows.

Purpose of the Speech

'Many of those who have spoken here in the past have praised the institution of this speech at the close of our ceremony. It seemed to them a mark of honour to our soldiers who have fallen in war that a speech should be made over them. I do not agree. These men have shown themselves valiant in action, and it would be enough, I think, for their glories to be proclaimed in action, as you have just seen it done at this funeral organized by the state. Our belief in the courage and manliness of so many should not be hazarded on the goodness or badness of one man's speech. Then it is not easy to speak with a proper sense of balance, when a man's listeners find it difficult to believe in the truth of what one is saying. The man who knows the facts and loves the dead may well think that an oration tells less than what he knows and what he would like to hear: others who do not know so much may feel envy for the dead, and think the orator over-praises them, when he speaks of exploits that are beyond their own capacities. Praise of other people is tolerable only up to a certain point, the point where one still believes that one could do oneself some of the things one is hearing about. Once you get beyond this point, you will find people becoming jealous and incredulous. However, the fact is that this institution was set up and approved by our forefathers, and it is my duty to follow the tradition and do my best to meet the wishes and the expectations of every one of you.

'I shall begin by speaking about our ancestors, since it is only right and proper on such an occasion to pay them the honour of recalling what they did. In this land of ours there have always been the same people living from generation to generation up till now, and they, by their courage and their virtues, have handed it on to us, a free country. They certainly deserve our praise. Even more so do our fathers deserve it. For to the inheritance they had received they added all the empire we have now, and it was not without blood and toil that they handed it down to us of the present generation. And then we ourselves, assembled here today, who are mostly in the prime of life, have, in most directions, added to the power of our empire and have organized our State in such a way that it is perfectly well able to look after itself both in peace and in war.

'I have no wish to make a long speech on subjects familiar to you all: so I shall say nothing about the warlike deeds by which we acquired our power or the battles in which we or our fathers gallantly resisted our enemies, Greek or foreign. What I want to do is, in the first place, to discuss the spirit in which we faced our trials and also our constitution and the way of life which has made us great. After that I shall speak in praise of the dead, believing that this kind of speech is not inappropriate to the present occasion, and that this whole assembly, of citizens and foreigners, may listen to it with advantage.

Democracy Is Power in the Hands of the People

'Let me say that our system of government does not copy the institutions of our neighbours. It is more the case of our being a model to others, than of our imitating anyone else. Our constitution is called a democracy because power is in the hands not of a minority but of the whole people. When it is a question of settling private disputes, everyone is equal before the law; when it is a question of putting one person before another in positions of public responsibility, what counts is not membership of a particular class, but the actual ability which the man possesses. No one, so long as he has it in him to be of service to the state, is kept in political obscurity because of poverty. And, just as our political life is free and open, so is our day-to-day life in our relations with each other. We do not get into a state with our next-door neighbour if he enjoys himself in his own way, nor do we give him the kind of black looks which, though they do no real harm, still do hurt people's feelings. We are free and tolerant in our private lives; but in public affairs we keep to the law. This is because it commands our deep respect.

'We give our obedience to those whom we put in positions of authority, and we obey the laws themselves, especially those which are for the protection of the oppressed, and those unwritten laws which it is an acknowledged shame to break.

'And here is another point. When our work is over, we are in a position to enjoy all kinds of recreation for our spirits. There are various kinds of contests and sacrifices regularly throughout the year; in our own homes we find a beauty and a good taste which delight us every day and which drive away our cares. Then the greatness of our city brings it about that all the good things from all over the world flow in to us, so that to us it seems just as natural to enjoy foreign goods as our own local products.

The Difference Between Athenians and Their Enemies

'Then there is a great difference between us and our opponents, in our attitude towards military security. Here are some examples: Our city is open to the world, and we have no periodical deportations in order to prevent people observing or finding out secrets which might be of military advantage to the enemy. This is because we rely, not on secret weapons, but on our own real courage and loyalty. There is a difference, too, in our educational systems. The Spartans, from their earliest boyhood, are submitted to the most laborious training in courage; we pass our lives without all these restrictions, and yet are just as ready to face the same dangers as they are. Here is a proof of this: When the Spartans invade our land, they do not come by themselves, but bring all their allies with them; whereas we, when we launch an attack abroad, do the job by ourselves, and, though fighting on foreign soil, do not often fail to defeat opponents who are fighting for their own hearths and homes. As a matter of fact none of our enemies has ever yet been confronted with our total strength, because we have to divide our attention between our navy and the many missions on which our troops are sent on land. Yet, if our enemies engage a detachment of our forces and defeat it, they give themselves credit for having thrown back our entire army; or, if they lose, they claim that they were beaten by us in full strength. There are certain advantages, I think, in our way of meeting danger voluntarily, with an easy mind, instead of with a laborious training, with natural rather than with state-induced courage. We do not have to spend our time practising to meet sufferings which are still in the future; and when they are actually upon us we show ourselves just as brave as these others who are always in strict training. This is one point in which, I think, our city deserves to be admired. There are also others:

'Our love of what is beautiful does not lead to extravagance; our love of the things of the mind does not make us soft. We regard wealth as something to be properly used, rather than as something to boast about. As for poverty, no one need be ashamed to admit it: the real shame is in not taking practical measures to escape from it. Here each individual is interested not only in his own affairs but in the affairs of the state as well: even those who are mostly occupied with their own business are extremely well-informed on general politics—this is a peculiarity of ours: we do not say that a man who takes no interest in politics is a man who minds his own business; we say that he has no business here at all. We Athenians, in our own persons, take our decisions on policy or submit them to proper discussions: for we do not think that there is an incompatibility between words and deeds; the worst thing is to rush into action before the consequences have been properly debated. And this is another point where we differ from other people. We are capable at the same time of taking risks and of estimating them beforehand. Others are brave out of ignorance; and, when they stop to think, they begin to fear. But the man who can most truly be accounted brave is he who best knows the meaning of what is sweet in life and of what is terrible, and then goes out undeterred to meet what is to come.

'Again, in questions of general good feeling there is a great contrast between us and most other people. We make friends by doing good to others, not by receiving good from them. This makes our friendship all the more reliable, since we want to keep alive the gratitude of those who are in our debt by showing continued goodwill to them: whereas the feelings of one who owes us something lack the same enthusiasm, since he knows that, when he repays our kindness, it will be more like paying back a debt than giving something spontaneously. We are unique in this. When we do kindnesses to others, we do not do them out of any calculations of profit or loss: we do them without afterthought, relying on our free liberality. Taking everything together then, I declare that our city is an education to Greece, and I declare that in my opinion each single one of our citizens, in all the manifold aspects of life, is able to show himself the rightful lord and owner of his own person, and do this, moreover, with exceptional grace and exceptional versatility. And to show that this is no empty boasting for the present occasion, but real tangible fact, you have only to consider the power which our city possesses and which has been won by those very qualities which I have mentioned. Athens, alone of the states we know, comes to her testing time in a greatness that surpasses what was imagined of her. In her case, and in her case alone, no invading enemy is ashamed at being defeated, and no subject can complain of being governed by people unfit for their responsibilities. Mighty indeed are the marks and monuments of our empire which we have left. Future ages will wonder at us, as the present age wonders at us now. We do not need the praises of a Homer, or of anyone else whose words may delight us for the moment, but whose estimation of facts will fall short of what is really true. For our adventurous spirit has forced an entry into every sea and into every land; and everywhere we have left behind us everlasting memorials of good done to our friends or suffering inflicted on our enemies.

'This, then, is the kind of city for which these men, who could not bear the thought of losing her, nobly fought and nobly died. It is only natural that every one of us who survive them should be willing to undergo hardships in her service. And it was for this reason that I have spoken at such length about our city, because I wanted to make it clear that for us there is more at stake than there is for others who lack our advantages; also I wanted my words of praise for the dead to be set in the bright light of evidence. And now the most important of these words has been spoken. I have sung the praises of our city; but it was the courage and gallantry of these men, and of people like them, which made her splendid. Nor would you find it true in the case of many of the Greeks, as it is true of them, that no words can do more than justice to their deeds.

In Praise of Those Who Died for the Greatness of Athens

'To me it seems that the consummation which has overtaken these men shows us the meaning of manliness in its first revelation and in its final proof. Some of them, no doubt, had their faults; but what we ought to remember first is their gallant conduct against the enemy in defence of their native land. They have blotted out evil with good, and done more service to the commonwealth than they ever did harm in their private lives. No one of these men weakened because he wanted to go on enjoying his wealth: no one put off the awful day in the hope that he might live to escape his poverty and grow rich. More to be desired than such things, they chose to check the enemy's pride. This, to them, was a risk most glorious, and they accepted it, willing to strike down the enemy and relinquish everything else. As for success or failure, they left that in the doubtful hands of Hope, and when the reality of battle was before their faces, they put their trust in their own selves. In the fighting, they thought it more honourable to stand their ground and suffer death than to give in and save their lives. So they fled from the reproaches of men, abiding with life and limb the brunt of battle; and, in a small moment of time, the climax of their lives, a culmination of glory, not of fear, were swept away from us.

'So and such they were, these men—worthy of their city. We who remain behind may hope to be spared their fate, but must resolve to keep the same daring spirit against the foe. It is not simply a question of estimating the advantages in theory. I could tell you a long story (and you know it as well as I do) about what is to be gained by beating the enemy back. What I would prefer is that you should fix your eyes every day on the greatness of Athens as she really is, and should fall in love with her. When you realize her greatness, then reflect that what made her great was men with a spirit of adventure, men who knew their duty, men who were ashamed to fall below a certain standard. If they ever failed in an enterprise, they made up their minds that at any rate the city should not find their courage lacking to her, and they gave to her the best contribution that they could. They gave her their lives, to her and to all of us, and for their own selves they won praises that never grow old, the most splendid of sepulchres—not the sepulchre in which their bodies are laid, but where their glory remains eternal in men's minds, always there on the right occasion to stir others to speech or to action. For famous men have the whole earth as their memorial: it is not only the inscriptions on their graves in their own country that mark them out; no, in foreign lands also, not in any visible form but in people's hearts, their memory abides and grows. It is for you to try to be like them. Make up your minds that happiness depends on being free, and freedom depends on being courageous. Let there be no relaxation in face of the perils of the war. The people who have most excuse for despising death are not the wretched and unfortunate, who have no hope of doing well for themselves, but those who run the risk of a complete reversal in their lives, and who would feel the difference most intensely, if things went wrong for them. Any intelligent man would find a humiliation caused by his own slackness more painful to bear than death, when death comes to him unperceived, in battle, and in the confidence of his patriotism.

'For these reasons I shall not commiserate with those parents of the dead, who are present here. Instead I shall try to comfort them. They are well aware that they have grown up in a world where there are many changes and chances. But this is good fortune—for men to end their lives with honour, as these have done, and for you honourably to lament them: their life was set to a measure where death and happiness went hand in hand. I know that it is difficult to convince you of this. When you see other people happy you will often be reminded of what used to make you happy too. One does not feel sad at not having some good thing which is outside one's experience: real grief is felt at the loss of something which one is used to. All the same, those of you who are of the right age must bear up and take comfort in the thought of having more children. In your own homes these new children will prevent you from brooding over those who are no more, and they will be a help to the city, too, both in filling the empty places, and in assuring her security. For it is impossible for a man to put forward fair and honest views about our affairs if he has not, like everyone else, children whose lives may be at stake. As for those of you who are now too old to have children, I would ask you to count as gain the greater part of your life, in which you have been happy, and remember that what remains is not long, and let your hearts be lifted up at the thought of the fair fame of the dead. One's sense of honour is the only thing that does not grow old, and the last pleasure, when one is worn out with age, is not, as the poet said, making money, but having the respect of one's fellow men.

'As for those of you here who are sons or brothers of the dead, I can see a hard struggle in front of you. Everyone always speaks well of the dead, and, even if you rise to the greatest heights of heroism, it will be a hard thing for you to get the reputation of having come near, let alone equalled, their standard. When one is alive, one is always liable to the jealousy of one's competitors, but when one is out of the way, the honour one receives is sincere and unchallenged.

'Perhaps I should say a word or two on the duties of women to those among you who are now widowed. I can say all I have to say in a short word of advice. Your great glory is not to be inferior to what God has made you, and the greatest glory of a woman is to be least talked about by men, whether they are praising you or criticizing you. I have now, as the law demanded, said what I had to say. For the time being our offerings to the dead have been made, and for the future their children will be supported at the public expense by the city, until they come of age. This is the crown and prize which she offers, both to the dead and to their children, for the ordeals which they bare faced. Where the rewards of valour are the greatest, there you will find also the best and bravest spirits among the people. And now, when you have mourned for your dear ones, you must depart.'

The Weakness of Democracy

Plato

The Republic *(ca. 360 BCE), regarded by many as the greatest work of Western philosophy, is Plato's treatise on the ideal political state. In the dialogue, Plato's teacher Socrates presents to several of his companions an account of the nature of justice, and in doing so describes what he thinks is the best form of government—a meritocracy in which a wise philosopher-king rules. He shows how other forms of government fail, and details where they go wrong. Democracy, which he views as "the extreme of popular liberty," he sees as a weak form of governance with the potential to collapse into tyranny. In the following excerpt from Book 8, Socrates explains how democracy arises from oligarchy. He describes the nature of democracy, and says that it is certainly the most attractive system of government. It offers wide freedoms, and people are regarded as equal whether they are or not. Socrates goes on to describe the character of the "democratic man," the lover of freedom and equality, who seeks pleasure, overindulges, and does not discern between what is desirable and what is good.*

'Our next subject, I suppose, is democracy. When we know how it originates, and what it is like, we can again identify and pass judgement on the corresponding individual.'

'That would be consistent with the procedure we've been following.'

How Oligarchy Changes into Democracy

'Then doesn't oligarchy change into democracy in the following way, as a result of lack of restraint in the pursuit of its objective of getting as rich as possible?'

'Tell me how.'

'Because the rulers, owing their power to wealth as they do, are unwilling to curtail by law the extravagance of the young, and prevent them squandering their money and ruining themselves; for it is by loans to such spendthrifts or by buying up their property that they hope to increase their own wealth and influence.'

'That's just what they want.'

'It should then be clear that love of money and adequate self-discipline in its citizens are two things that can't coexist in any society; one or the other must be neglected.'

'That's pretty clear.'

'This neglect and the encouragement of extravagance in an oligarchy often reduces to poverty men born for better things.'

'Yes, often.'

'Some of them are in debt, some disfranchised, some both, and they settle down, armed with their stings, and with hatred in their hearts, to plot against those who have deprived them of their property and against the rest of society, and to long for revolution.'

'Yes, they do.'

'Meanwhile the money-makers, bent on their business, don't appear to notice them, but continue to inject their poisoned loans wherever they can find a victim, and to demand high rates of interest on the sum lent, with the result that the drones and beggars multiply.'

'A result that's bound to follow.'

'Yet even when the evil becomes flagrant they will do nothing to quench it, either by preventing men from disposing of their property as they like, or alternatively by other suitable legislation.'

'What legislation?'

'It's only a second best, but it does compel some respect for decent behaviour. If contracts for a loan were, in general, made by law at the lender's risk, there would be a good deal less shameless money-making and a good deal less of the evils I have been describing.'

'Much less.'

'But as it is the oligarchs reduce their subjects to the state we have described, while as for themselves and their dependents—their young men live in luxury and idleness, physical and mental, become idle, and lose their ability to resist pain or pleasure.'

'Indeed they do.'

'And they themselves care for nothing but making money, and have no greater concern for excellence than the poor.'

'True.'

'Such being the state of rulers and ruled, what will happen when they come up against each other in the streets or in the course of business, at a festival or on a campaign, serving in the navy or army? When they see each other in moments of danger, the rich man will no longer be able to despise the poor man; the poor man will be lean and sunburnt, and find himself fighting next to some rich man whose sheltered life and superfluous flesh make him puff and blow and quite unable to cope. Won't he conclude that people like this are rich because their subjects are cowards, and won't he say to his fellows, when he meets them in private, "This lot are no good; we've got them where we want them"?'

'I'm quite sure he will.'

'When a person's unhealthy, it takes very little to upset him and make him ill; there may even be an internal cause for disorder. The same is true of an unhealthy society. It will fall into sickness and dissension at the slightest external provocation, when one party or the other calls in help from a neighbouring oligarchy or democracy; while sometimes faction fights will start without any external stimulus at all.'

'Very true.'

'Then democracy originates when the poor win, kill or exile their opponents, and give the rest equal civil rights and opportunities of office, appointment to office being as a rule by lot.

'Yes,' he agreed, 'that is how a democracy is established, whether it's done by force of arms or by frightening its opponents into withdrawal.'

What Sort of Society Will Democracy Produce?

'What sort of a society will it be?' I asked, 'and how will its affairs be run? The answer, obviously, will show us the character of the democratic man.'

'Obviously.'

'Would you agree, first, that people will be free? There is liberty and freedom of speech in plenty, and every individual is free to do as he likes.'

'That's what they say.'

'Granted that freedom, won't everyone arrange his life as pleases him best?'

'Obviously.'

'And so there will be in this society the greatest variety of individual character?'

'There's bound to be.'

'I dare say that a democracy is the most attractive of all societies,' I said. 'The diversity of its characters, like the different colours in a patterned dress, make it look very attractive. Indeed,' I added, 'perhaps most people would, for this reason, judge it to be the best form of society, like women and children when they see gaily coloured things.'

'Very likely.'

'And, you know, it's just the place to go constitution-hunting.'

'How so?'

'It contains every possible type, because of the wide freedom it allows, and anyone engaged in founding a state, as we are doing, should perhaps be made to pay a visit to a democracy and choose what he likes from the variety of models it displays, before he proceeds to make his own foundation.'

'It's a shop in which he'd find plenty of models on show.'

'Then in democracy,' I went on, 'there's no compulsion either to exercise authority if you are capable of it, or to submit to authority if you don't want to; you needn't fight if there's a war, or you can wage a private war in peacetime if you don't like peace; and if there's any law that debars you from political or judicial office, you will none the less take either if they come your way. It's a wonderfully pleasant way of carrying on in the short run, isn't it?

'In the short run perhaps.'

'And isn't there something rather charming about the good-temper of those who've been sentenced in court? You must have noticed that in a democracy men sentenced to death or exile stay on, none the less, and go about among their fellows, with no more notice taken of their comings and goings than if they were invisible spirits.'

'I've often seen that.'

'Then they're very considerate in applying the high principles we laid down when founding our state; so far from interpreting them strictly, they really look down on them. We said that no one who had not exceptional gifts could grow into a good man unless he were brought up from childhood in a good environment and trained in good habits. Democracy with a grandiose gesture sweeps all this away and doesn't mind what the habits and background of its politicians are; provided they profess themselves the people's friends, they are duly honoured.'

'All very splendid.'

'These, then, and similar characteristics are those of democracy. It's an agreeable anarchic form of society, with plenty of variety, which treats all men as equal, whether they are equal or not.'

'The description is easy to recognize.'

The Democratic Character

'Then let us look at the corresponding individual. Should we first look at his origin, as we did with the society?'

'Yes.'

'Won't it be like this? Our mean oligarchic character may have a son, whom he will bring up in his own ways.'

'So far, so good.'

'He will forcibly restrain himself from those pleasures that lead to expense rather than profit, the "unnecessary" pleasures as they have been called.'

'Yes, obviously.'

'Then do you think that, if we are to avoid arguing in the dark, we had better define the difference between necessary and unnecessary desires?'

'Yes, I think so.'

'Desires we can't avoid, or whose satisfaction benefits us, can fairly be called necessary, I think. We are bound by our very nature to want to satisfy both, are we not?'

'Certainly.'

'And so may surely with justice use the term "necessary" to describe them.'

'Yes.'

'But we can call "unnecessary" all desires which can be got rid of with practice, if we start young, and whose presence either does us no good or positive harm. Isn't that a fair enough description?'

'Fair enough.'

'Shall we give examples of each, to get a general idea of what we mean?'

'I think we should.'

'Would you say that the desire to eat enough for health and fitness, and the desire for the bread and meat requisite for the purpose, was necessary?'

'Yes, I think so.'

'And the desire for bread is necessary on both counts, because it benefits us and because it is indispensable to life.'

'Yes.'

'And the desire for meat so far as it conduces to fitness.'

'Certainly.'

'But the desire for a more varied and luxurious diet is one which, with discipline and training from an early age, can normally be got rid of, and which is physically harmful and psychologically damaging to intelligence and self-discipline. May it not therefore rightly be called unnecessary?'

'Quite rightly.'

'The first kind of desire we could also call acquisitive, because of its practical usefulness, the second kind wasteful.'

'True.'

'And does not the same hold good of sex and the other desires?'

'Yes.'

'Then what we called the drone type will, as we said, be swayed by a mass of such unnecessary pleasures and desires, the thrifty oligarchic type by necessary ones.'

'Yes.'

'Let's go back to the question how the democratic man originates from the oligarchic. This generally happens, I think, as follows.'

'How?'

'When a young man, brought up in the narrow economical way we have described, gets a taste of the drones' honey and gets into brutal and dangerous company, where he can be provided with every variety and refinement of pleasure, with the result that his internal oligarchy starts turning into a democracy.'

'That's bound to happen.'

'In society the change took place when one party brought in sympathizers from outside to help it. Will the change in our young man be brought about when one or other type of desire in him gets assistance from kindred and similar desires outside him?'

'Yes, certainly.'

'And I take it that if the oligarchic element in him gets support from a counter-alliance of the remonstrances and criticisms either of his father or of other members of his family, the result is a conflict of factions and a battle between the two parts of himself.'

'True enough.'

'And sometimes the democratic element gives way to the oligarchic, and some of his desires are destroyed and some driven out; and a certain sense of decency is produced in the young man's mind and internal order restored.'

'Yes, that sometimes happens.'

'Alternatively the exiled desires are succeeded by others akin to them, which are nursed in secret because of his father's ignorance of how to bring him up properly, and grow in number and strength.'

'This is the normal course of events.'

'These drag him back to his old associates, and breed and multiply in secret.'

'True again.'

'In the end they capture the seat of government, having discovered that the young man's mind is devoid of sound knowledge and practices and true principles, the most effective safeguards the mind of man can be blessed with.'

'Far the most effective.'

'The vacant citadel in the young man's mind is filled instead by an invasion of pretentious fallacies and opinions.'

'Very much so.'

'And back he goes to live with the Lotus-eaters. If his family send help to the economical element in him, the pretentious invaders shut the gates of the citadel, and will not admit the relieving force, nor will they listen to the individual representations of old and trusted friends. They make themselves masters by force of arms, they call shame silliness and drive it into disgrace and exile; they call self-control cowardice and expel it with abuse; and they call on a lot of useless desires to help them banish economy and moderation, which they maintain are mere provincial parsimony.'

'All very true.'

'They expel the lot and leave the soul of their victim swept clean, ready for the great initiation which follows, when they lead in a splendid garlanded procession of insolence, licence, extravagance, and shamelessness. They praise them all extravagantly and call insolence good breeding, licence liberty, extravagance generosity, and shamelessness courage. Do you agree,' I asked, 'that that's how a young man brought up in the necessary desires comes to throw off all inhibitions and indulge desires that are unnecessary and useless?'

'Yes, your description is very clear.'

'For the rest of his life he spends as much money, time and trouble on the unnecessary desires as on the necessary. If he's lucky and doesn't get carried to extremes, the tumult will subside as he gets older, some of the exiles will be received back, and the invaders won't have it all their own way. He'll establish a kind of equality of pleasures, and will give the pleasure of the moment its turn of complete control till it is satisfied, and then move on to another, so that none is underprivileged and all have their fair share of encouragement.'

'That's true.'

'If anyone tells him that some pleasures, because they spring from good desires, are to be encouraged and approved, and others, springing from evil desires, to be disciplined and repressed, he won't listen or open his citadel's doors to the truth, but shakes his head and says all pleasures are equal and should have equal rights.'

'Yes, that's just how he feels and just what he does.'

'In fact,' I said, 'he lives from day to day, indulging the pleasure of the moment. One day it's wine, women and song, the next water to drink and a strict diet; one day it's hard physical training, the next indolence and careless ease, and then a period of philosophic study. Often he takes to politics and keeps jumping to his feet and saying or doing whatever comes into his head. Sometimes all his ambitions and efforts are military, sometimes they are all directed to success in business. There's no order or restraint in his life, and he reckons his way of living is pleasant, free and happy, and sticks to it through thick and thin.'

'A very good description of the life of one who believes in liberty and equality,' he commented.

'Yes,' I said, 'and I think that the versatility of the individual, and the attractiveness of his combination of a wide variety of characteristics, match the variety of the democratic society. It's a life which many men and women would envy, it contains patterns of so many constitutions and ways of life.'

'It does indeed.'

'This, then, is the individual corresponding to the democratic society, and we can fairly call him the democratic man.'

'Agreed.'

The Lessons of
Ancient Democracy

C.L.R. James

Born in the colony of Trinidad and Tobago, C.L.R. (Cyril Lionel Robert) James (1901–1989) was a journalist, teacher, historian dramatist, fiction writer, and socialist theorist. A committed Marxist, he campaigned for independence for the West Indies and Trinidad and championed Pan-Africanism, a political movement concerned with the uniting of all Africans. Having been educated in the classics in Trinidad, James was keenly interested in the ancient world and questions raised by the civilization of the Greeks. In the following excerpt, he argues that the greatest lesson of the Athenian democracy for the modern world is that when every citizen is governed equally and when equality is carried to its extreme, the city produces the most varied, comprehensive, and brilliant body of geniuses. According to James, in Athenian society ordinary people were not exploited and thus they were able to create a world where, in a phrase that he borrowed from the Russian Communist leader Vladimir Lenin, "every cook can govern."

The Greek form of government was the city-state. Every Greek city was an independent state. At its best, in the city-state of Athens, the public assembly of all the citizens made all important decisions on such questions as peace or war. They listened to the envoys of foreign powers and decided what their attitude should be to what these foreign powers had sent to say. They dealt with all serious questions of taxation, they appointed the generals who should lead them in time of war. They organized the administration of the state, appointed officials and kept check on them. The public assembly of all the citizens was the government.

C.L.R. James, "Every Cook Can Govern," *Correspondence*, vol. 2, no. 12, June 1956. Reproduced by permission.

Perhaps the most striking thing about Greek Democracy was that the administration (and there were immense administrative problems) was organized upon the basis of what is known as sortition, or, more easily, selection by lot. The vast majority of Greek officials were chosen by a method which amounted to putting names into a hat and appointing the ones whose names came out.

Now the average CIO [Congress of Industrial Organizations labor organization] bureaucrat or Labor Member of Parliament in Britain would fall in a fit if it was suggested to him that any worker selected at random could do the work that he is doing, but that was precisely the guiding principle of Greek Democracy. . . . Before the democracy came into power, the Greeks had been governed by various forms of government, including government by representatives. The democracy knew representative government and rejected it. It refused to believe that the ordinary citizen was not able to perform practically all the business of government. Not only did the public assembly of all the citizens keep all the important decisions in its own hands. For the Greek, the word *isonomia*, which meant equality, was used interchangeably for democracy. For the Greek, the two meant the same thing. For the Greek, a man who did not take part in politics was an *idiotes*, an idiot, from which we get our modern word idiot, whose meaning, however, we have limited. Not only did the Greeks choose all officials by lot, they limited their time of service. When a man had served once, as a general rule, he was excluded from serving again because the Greeks believed in rotation, everybody taking his turn to administer the state.

Intellectuals' Concerns Direct Democracy

Intellectuals like Plato and Aristotle detested the system. And Socrates thought that government should be by experts and not by the common people. For centuries, philosophers and political writers, bewildered by these Greeks who when they said equality meant it, have either abused this democracy or tried to explain that this direct democracy was suitable only for the city-state. Large modern communities, they say, are unsuitable for such a form of government.

We of *Correspondence* [radical publishing organization founded by James] believe that the larger the modern community, the more imperative it is for it to govern itself by the principle of direct democracy (it need not be a mere copy of the Greek). Otherwise we face a vast and ever-growing bureaucracy. That is why a study, however brief of the constitution and governmental procedures of Greek Democracy is so important for us today. Let us see how Greek Democracy administered justice. The Greek cities for a time had special magistrates and judges of a special type, like those that we have today. When the democracy came into power, about the middle of the 5th Century BCE, there began and rapidly developed a total reorganization of the system of justice. The quorum for important sessions of the assembly was supposed to be 6,000. The Greek Democracy therefore at the beginning of each year, chose by lot 12 groups of 500 each. These 500 tried the cases and their decisions were final. The Greek Democracy made the magistrate or the judge into a mere clerk of the court. He took the preliminary information and he presided as an official during the case. But his position as presiding officer was merely formal. The jury did not, as in our courts today, decide only on the facts and look to him for information on the law. They decided on the law as well as on the facts. Litigants pleaded their own case, though a litigant could go to a man learned in the law, get him to write a speech and read it himself. The Greeks were great believers in law, both written and unwritten. But the democrats believed not only in the theory of law, but in the principles of equity and we can define equity as what would seem right in a given case in the minds of 500 citizens chosen by lot from among the Athenian population.

Experts Are Unnecessary

He would be a very bold man who would say that that system of justice was in any way inferior to the modern monstrosities by which lawyers mulct [defraud] the public, cases last interminably, going from court to court, and matters of grave importance are decided by the position of full stops and commas (or the absence of them) in long and complicated laws and regulations which sometimes have to be traced through hundreds of years and hundreds of law books. When the Russian Revolution took place and was in its heroic period, the Bolsheviks experimented with People's Courts. But they were timid and in any case, none of these experiments lasted for very long. The essence of the Greek method, here as elsewhere, was the refusal to hand over these things to experts, but to trust to the intelligence and sense of justice of the population at large, which meant of course a majority of the common people.

The Organization of Government

We must get rid of the idea that there was anything primitive in the organization of the government of Athens. On the contrary, it was a miracle of democratic procedure which would be beyond the capacity of any modern body of politicians and lawyers, simply because these believe that when every man has a vote, equality is thereby established. The assembly appointed a council of 500 to be responsible for the administration of the city and the carrying out of decisions.

But the council was governed by the same principle of equality. The city was divided into 10 divisions and the year was divided into 10 periods. Each section of the city selected by lot 50 men to serve on the council. All the councillors of each section held office for one tenth of the year. So that 50 people were always in charge of the administration. The order in which the group of 50 councillors from each section of the city should serve was determined by lot. Every day, the 50 who were serving chose someone to preside over them and he also was chosen by lot. If on the day that he was presiding, the full assembly met, he presided at the assembly.

The council had a secretary and he was elected. But he was elected only for the duration of one tenth of the year. And (no doubt to prevent bureaucracy) he was elected not from among the 50, but from among the 450 members of the council who were not serving at the time.

When members had served on the council, they were forbidden to serve a second time. Thus every person had a chance to serve. And here we come to one of the great benefits of the system. After a number of years, practically every citizen had had an opportunity to be a member of the administration. So that the body of citizens who formed the public assembly consisted of men who were familiar with the business of government.

No business could be brought before the assembly except it had been previously prepared and organized by the council.

When decisions had been taken, the carrying out of them was entrusted to the council. The council supervised all the magistrates and any work that had been given to a private citizen to do.

The Greeks had very few permanent functionaries. They preferred to appoint special boards of private citizens. Each of these boards had its own very carefully defined sphere of work. The coordination of all these various spheres of work was carried out by the council. A great number of special commissions helped to carry out the executive work. For example, there were 10 members of a commission to see after naval affairs, and 10 members of a commission to hear complaints against magistrates at the end of their term. One very interesting commission was the commission for the conduct of religious ceremonies. The Greeks were a very religious people. But most of the priests and officials of the temples were elected and were for the most part private citizens. The

Greeks would not have any bunch of Bishops, Archbishops, Popes and other religious bureaucrats who lived by organizing religion. Some of these commissions were elected from the council. But others again were appointed by lot.

At every turn we see the extraordinary confidence that these people had in the ability of the ordinary person, the grocer, the candlestick maker, the carpenter, the sailor, the tailor. Whatever the trade of the individual, whatever his education, he was chosen by lot to do the work the state required.

And yet they stood no nonsense. If a private individual made propositions in the assembly which the assembly considered frivolous or stupid, the punishment was severe.

Democratic Drama

Here is some idea of the extent to which the Greeks believed in democracy and equality. One of the greatest festivals in Greece, or rather in Athens, was the festival of Dionysus, the climax of which was the performance of plays for four days, from sunrise to evening. The whole population came out to listen. Officials chose the different playwrights who were to compete. On the day of the performance, the plays were performed and, as far as we can gather, the prizes were at first given by popular applause and the popular vote. You must remember that the dramatic companies used to rehearse for one year and the successful tragedians were looked upon as some of the greatest men in the state, receiving immense honor and homage from their fellow citizens. Yet it was the public, the general public, of 15 or 20 thousand people that came and decided who was the winner.

Later, a committee was appointed to decide. Today such a committee would consist of professors, successful writers and critics. Not among the Greeks. The committee consisted first of a certain number of men chosen by lot from each section of the city. These men got together and chose by lot from among themselves 10 men. These 10 men attended as the judges. At the end of the performances, they made their decision. The 10 decisions were placed in the hat. Five were drawn out. And the one who had the highest vote from among these five received the prize. But even that does not give a true picture of the attitude of the Greeks towards democracy.

Despite the appointment of this commission, there is evidence that the spectators had a preponderant influence on the judges. The Greek populace behaved at these dramatic competitions as a modern crowd behaves at some football or baseball game. They were violent partisans. They stamped and shouted and showed their likes and dislikes in those and similar ways. We are told that the judges took good care to notice the way in which popular opinion went. Because, and this is typical of the whole working of the democracy on the day after the decision, the law allowed dissatisfied citizens to impeach the members of the commission for unsatisfactory decisions. So that the members of the commission (we can say at least) were very much aware of the consequences of 15 disregarding the popular feeling about the plays.

Yet it was the Greeks who invented playwriting. In Aeschylus, Sophocles and Euripides, they produced three tragedians who, to this day, have no equals as practitioners of the art which they invented. Aristophanes has never been surpassed as a writer of Comic plays.

These men obviously knew that to win the prize, they had to please the populace. Plato, the great philosopher, was, as can easily be imagined, extremely hostile to this method of decision. But the Greek populace gave the prize to Aeschylus 13 times. They were the ones who repeatedly crowned Aeschylus and Sophocles, and later Euripides, as prize winners. It is impossible to see how a jury consisting of Plato and his philosopher friends could have done any better. There you have a perfect example of the Greek attitude to the capacities, judgment and ability to represent the whole body of citizens, which they thought existed in every single citizen.

Democracy Is Not an Ancient Western Concept

Raul S. Manglapus

Raul S. Manglapus was a prominent Filipino politician and lawyer. He was a popular senator in the Philippines and became foreign secretary under President Corazon Aquino. In Will of the People: Original Democracy in Non-Western Societies, *Manglapus argues that democracy is not a Western concept but "a value that has been treasured and practiced in the East—in Asia, the Middle East and elsewhere—as far back as at least 2500 BCE." He uses case studies from Asia, the Middle East, Africa, and the Americas to show that democracy has been the natural state of most of mankind throughout history. He claims it was practiced in the earliest tribes and villages through discussion, consensus, and customary law. In the following chapter, Manglapus contends that the earliest formal democracy gradually developed in Mesopotamia, today's Iraq, between 2500 and 4000 BCE. Citing archaeological evidence, he shows that Mesopotamians elected their officials and held egalitarian values. Their basic and somewhat crude form of democracy, says Manglapus, not only resembles modern Swiss, American, and British systems, but in some ways was actually superior.*

In searching East and West for original democratic traditions, one need not retreat when confronted with monarchy, aristocracy, nobility, or slavery. In fact, the search must begin in the East, not the West, for it is in the East that early original egalitarian societies first developed hierarchies and

Raul S. Manglapus, "Mesopotamia: Earliest Formal Democracy?" *Will of the People: Original Democracy in Non-Western Societies*, Westport, CT: Greenwood Press, 1987.

blossomed into mature civilizations, clustered around life-giving sources of water which provided not only irrigation but also arteries of commerce and communication, stimulating urbanization.

In fact, the earliest such civilization, Mesopotamia, was named for its position between the two great rivers Tigris and Euphrates (Greek *mesos*, middle, and *potamos*, river). It is the earliest prototype for [historian Karl A.] Wittfogel's "hydraulic society," which necessitates and produces Oriental despotic power—"total and not benevolent." Indeed the most common recollections of Mesopotamia are those of original imperial despotisms.

Nature of the Original Mesopotamian Societies

However, the story of the birth of an empire, focusing on the forces that it took to weld it out of scattered communities, may not bother to look into the character of the original communities. It was, in fact, the search for steady irrigation that brought farming communities to the alluvial lowlands of the Tigris-Euphrates system around 4000 BCE In apparent contradiction of the Wittfogel theory, there was no spontaneous growth of centralized despotism among them—only villages that "were relatively self-sufficient and politically autonomous." Five hundred years later, they developed their first cities, and still 500 years later they put together the first known system of handwriting.

At that point, [cultural anthropologist Elman R.] Service points out, "we merge archaeology (prehistory) with documentary history. It is documentary history that tells us of life and government in the Mesepotamian cities."

A. Leo Oppenheim writes of the coexistence of two components in Mesopotamian society, in a "pattern (which) maintained its effectiveness through three millennia." First there was the community of persons of equal status bound together by a consciousness of belonging, realized by directing their communal affairs by means of an assembly, in which, under a presiding officer, some measure of consensus was reached as it was the case in the rich and quasi-independent old cities of Babylonia.

Side by side with this democratic configuration there was a second "organization of persons entirely different in structure and temperament from the community just mentioned, whose center and raison dêtre [justification for existence] was either the temple or the palace, either the household of the deity or that of the king." Here, then, we have an early instance of a kingdom, within the tight confines of its city-state where the population was within reach of the royal power, which not only tolerated but complemented an operative popular sovereignty. "The solidarity of a Mesopotamian city," observes Oppenheim, "is reflected in the absence of any status or ethnic or tribal articulation." The community of citizens "constituted as an assembly" not only administered the city under a presiding official but also made legal decisions, some of them ceremonially confirmed by the king. Its coexistence with the temple-palace system created for the Mesopotamian city "an equilibrium of forces and an overall harmony that endowed the city with the longevity which the Greek Polis could not achieve."

However, it is another anthropologist, Thorkild Jacobsen, who provides us with deeper, and more sanguine, insights into the democratic character of Ancient Mesopotamia. Jacobsen read a paper entitled, "Primitive Democracy in Ancient Mesopotamia" at the meeting of the American Oriental Society in Chicago in April 1941. His "primitive democracy" is more substance than form, where "sovereignty resides in the citizens," but "the various functions of government are as yet little specialized, the power structure is loose, and the machinery for social coordination is as yet imperfectly developed." He then portrays a Mesopotamia where the classic historical confrontation between democratic and autocratic tendencies takes place. The autocratic drive was strong: "The country formed a mosaic of diminutive, self-sufficient, autonomous city-states, and in each such state one individual, the ruler, united in his hands the chief political powers: legislative, judiciary, and executive." This autocratic momentum "drove Mesopotamia forward relentlessly toward the more distant aim: centralization of power within one large area." Lugal-Zaggisi achieved this goal with his "activities imperial," followed by King Sargon and the highly organized bureaucratic state of the Third nasty of Ur.

Evidence of Democratic Institutions

Working its way up against this autocratic downstream was the egalitarian [desire for equal rights for all people] instinct of the original society, producing seemingly anachronistic [chronologically misplaced] democratic institutions. In Assyria the highest judicial authority was a general assembly of all colonists: *karumir sahir rabi*—"the colony young and old"— which could be called into session by a clerk only at the bidding of a majority of its senior members. If the clerk issued the call at the request of only one individual, he was fined ten shekels of silver! Besides discharging judicial functions, the general assembly had its political duties. For example, it could overrule objections of particular colonists to the coming of commissaries sent by the legal authorities of the mother-city Assur.

In Babylonia, where "we are very naturally struck first of all by the degree to which royal power is there in evidence" anyone had recourse directly to the king for redress, and he could delegate each case to suitable courts for decision. But alongside the king and his judicial powers stood "the Babylonian city," whose town mayor and town elders settled minor disputes and where the whole town—*Puhrum*, the "assembly"—decided important cases "according to its own local ideas of right and wrong."

To prove that the participation in the *Puhrum* and its judicial function was not limited to a favored class but was open, perhaps with some degree of compulsion, to all citizens, Jacobsen quotes a Babylonian proverb which presages modern-day counsel from stand-up comedians to potential witness summons dodgers and jury-duty evaders:

Do not go stand in the assembly.

Do not stray to the very place of strife.

It is precisely in strife that fate may overtake you;

Besides, you may be made a witness for them.

So that they take you along to testify in a lawsuit not your own.

Jacobsen believes that these democratic judicial institutions were not the vanguard of a vigorous democratic thrust but rather "a last stronghold, a stubborn survival, of ideas rooted in earlier ages." Thus, perhaps unwittingly, he refutes those who, while ostensibly advocating support of democracy for all nations, insist that it can only come with growth, progress, and development.

As Jacobsen looks backward in time at Mesopotamian history, "the competence and influence of the 'assembly' appears to grow and to extend from judiciary functions to other, even more vital, aspects of government." In the days of the kings of Akkad, "the assembly deemed it within its authority to choose a king." Farther back in older tradition concerning Uruk in the time of Gilgamesh, "beyond the border line of history proper," the ruler consults the assembly in important matters of peace and war. Gilgamesh, lord of Uruk, is remembered as consulting first the senate, "the elders of Uruk," and then the assembly, "the men of the town," before he decides to arm for a fight with King Agga of Kish. His consultation is not only for advice but for consent, and, Jacobsen correctly concludes, the assembly is recognized as "the ultimate political authority."

Egalitarianism in Religion's Legends

The success of the early Mesopotamian democratic thrust appears to be traceable to the fact that the egalitarian values of the primitive population were successfully translated into religious legend.

The Sumerians and the Akkadians projected their human terrestrial conditions into their world of gods and goddesses, who reflected early Mesopotamian culture by organizing themselves politically along democratic lines. There was, according to the Adad myth, an assembly of gods and goddesses usually held in a large court called *Ubshuukkinna*.

An, the god of heaven and "father of the gods," was their presiding officer, and Enlil, god of the storm, was their executive officer and discussion leader. There were fifty "senior gods"—corresponding to the earthly seniors of the Assyrian *karum*—who handled the discussion, and seven deciding "gods of fates," corresponding to the group of seven members of the *karum* entitled to seal documents.

The assembly's functions were not only judicial. It also had the authority to grant kingship and to take it back. The period of kingship was called *bala*, the same word applied to the term of earthly Sumerian kings and—in its altered form *palu*—to that of the rulers of Akkad.

The elections of Mesopotamian kings of that period were dramatically confirmed as late as 1976 by the excavations which yielded the remains of the lost kingdom of Ebla, which flourished in 2500 BCE, [according to Chaim Bermant and Michael Weitzman] a "large and thriving commercial, administrative, and intellectual center with economic and political institutions that sound remarkably familiar."

Elected Officials

The diggings yielded some 15,000 clay tablets or fragments written in Sumerian cuneiform. The king of Ebla, according to the records discovered in the palace archives, was elected for a seven-year term and shared power with a council of elders. The king (we would probably call him President today) who lost reelection bids retired on a government pension!

What is involved here is not a primitive, prehierarchical society or a hierarchical society of limited scope—such as a village or even a town or city-state. Ebla, whose existence had long been inferred from Mesopotamian literature, now rises in history, through its own records, as a fairly extended kingdom of at least 250,000 inhabitants—a large population in those days—with a capital city of 30,000 residents "of whom eleven thousand seven hundred were civil servants." It was a society of highly organized sophistication. The findings included Sumerian-Eblaite dictionaries of more than 3,000 words, expense accounts of traveling diplomats, and even a list of beers, one of which was called *ebla*, "pronounced just like the city," write Bermant and Weitzman, venturing to add the obvious observation "could it have been the beer that made Ebla famous?"

Ebla appears to have hosted international conferences and dominated many other kingdoms and cities politically and economically. Among its principal trading partners were the cities of Sodom and Gomorrah, whose historical reality had been doubted until now.

So the thrust of Mesopotamian democracy, which even its enthusiastic commentator Jacobsen would cautiously trace as a declining tradition from "beyond the border line of history proper," now receives even stronger confirmation in recorded history than that which already had been found for it by Jacobsen and, after him, Oppenheim.

A little less than 4,000 years before the maturing of British Parliamentarism, the founding of the Swiss Confederation, and the birth of the American republic, we find in Mesopotamia a likeness of a political system which, although with much cruder and broader strokes of the brush, strikingly resembles the finer lines of the Swiss and American written constitutions and the unwritten charter of the British system.

On one fine but crucial point the Mesopotamian democracy may have been superior to at least the current Swiss system. The *Puhrum*, or assembly of the Babylonian gods, was open to goddesses. An old Babylonian hymn, the song of the goddess Ishtar, relates that "in their (i.e., the gods') assembly her word is highly esteemed, is surpassing; she sits among them counting as much (with them) as Anum, their king." If the reality of the Babylonian system was, as we have seen above, but a reflection of the democratic legends of the Babylonian deities, then women may have participated in the earthly *Puhrum*. In Switzerland, women received the right to vote in the constitution only in 1971, and up to this writing they may not vote or even participate in some cantons in those open-air, popular assemblies for which Switzerland has had such a rightful claim to fame.

The Eblan discovery, as well as the Oppenheim and Jacobsen theses, may now enable us to cross the line between substance and form. As we move from the cradle of civilization to its neighbor, India, we may perhaps begin to feel entitled to suspect that, whether in form or substance, democracy may have been, indeed, the natural state of early man wherever he may have been.

CHAPTER 2

American Democracy

Chapter Preface

When the United States was established as a nation in the late eighteenth century, it was seen as one of the most extraordinary and radical political systems in existence. Not since the Romans had a republic been founded in which authority was truly in the hands of the people. However, the United States was not formally a democracy, nor did the people who governed it want it to be. The Founding Fathers feared that democracy would degenerate into despotism—which is exactly what they had sought to escape in establishing the new nation. Thus they set up the United States as a constitutional republic with three coequal branches—executive, legislative, and judicial—to protect individual rights and an intricate system of checks and balances to ensure that no one branch oversteps its bounds.

Although the founders were suspicious of the direct democracy characteristic of the ancient Greek city-states, the Declaration of Independence does in fact set forth principles that most people now equate with democracy: freedom, equality, individual rights, and popular sovereignty. But while these values were stated in the Declaration and other early documents, many historians and cultural critics have argued that democracy in the United States was actually the result of a process that took several centuries, and not something that was established with the overthrow of British rule.

When the Frenchman Alexis de Tocqueville, who visited the United States in the 1830s, wrote his classic study, *Democracy in America* in 1835, for example, American democracy still included slavery and excluded the poor and women from voting. When President Andrew Jackson extended democracy to the common people, he was reviled by many, including John Quincy Adams. Ironically, it was Adams who later became an abolitionist even as Jackson supported slavery. Principles of democracy were a point of contention during the Civil War. In his important speech at Gettysburg at a turning point in the war, Abraham Lincoln reinterpreted the U.S. Constitution to make equality the right not just of those already free, but of free and slave alike in what he called a "new birth of freedom."

Including others into the fold of those who are equal and free, however, continued to be a struggle. It was not until 1920 that women were granted voting rights. Nonwhites were awarded voting rights with ratification of the Fifteenth Amendment to the Constitution in 1870, but had to wait until the bitter battle of the Civil Rights Movement in the 1960s before full voting rights were granted to blacks. In the 1940s African American poet Langston Hughes noted the irony of his lack of rights in the land of the free, lamenting: "I swear to the Lord / I still can't see / Why Democracy means / Everybody but me." The fight to secure complete voting rights for blacks was only won after a bitter battle in the 1960s.

The nature of American democracy continues to evolve, but many recent commentators have expressed dismay at what they see as the erosion of fundamental rights and thus the trampling of American democracy in the United States in recent years. Since the September 11, 2001, terrorist attacks on the United States, legislation has been enacted that has impinged on citizens' freedoms, these critics say. The government has sought to justify these restrictions on Americans' freedom by arguing that it is necessary in the "war against terror." The USA Patriot Act, for example, amends laws that allow the government to monitor electronic communications and search businesses for information gathering related to possible terrorist activities. Such policies, it is argued, have diminished American democracy. Other commentators, however, see these developments as safeguarding the United States from potential terrorist attacks.

Government Derives Its Power from the Consent of the Governed

Thomas Jefferson

Drafted by Thomas Jefferson in June 1776, the Declaration of Independence is the most prized symbol of freedom of the United States and the root of American democracy. In the document, Jefferson, one of the framers of the U.S. Constitution, expresses the ideals of individual liberty that had been discussed by John Locke and other political philosophers. He summarizes this philosophy in "self-evident truths" and sets forth a list of grievances against the king in order to justify the independence of the thirteen American colonies from England. The Declaration contains within it the guiding principles of American democracy: that all people are created equal; that the purpose of government is to protect the individual rights and property of the people; that the power of government is with and from the people and can be overthrown when it fails to fulfill its obligations; that every person accused of a crime is entitled to trial by a jury of peers; that the state cannot search the homes of its citizens without a warrant; that the government controls the army and not the reverse; and that there should be no taxation without representation. The development of American democracy, it has been said, is an elucidation of the premises outlined in the Declaration.

In Congress, July 4, 1776.

The unanimous Declaration of the thirteen united States of America,

Thomas Jefferson, in the Declaration of Independence, 1776.

When in the Course of human events, it becomes necessary for one people to dissolve the political bands which have connected them with another, and to assume among the powers of the earth, the separate and equal station to which the Laws of Nature and of Nature's God entitle them, a decent respect to the opinions of mankind requires that they should declare, the causes which impel them to the separation.

We hold these truths to be self-evident, that all men are created equal, that they are endowed by their Creator with certain unalienable Rights, that among these are Life, Liberty and the pursuit of Happiness—That to secure these rights, Governments are instituted among Men, deriving their just powers from the consent of the governed,—That whenever any Form of Government becomes destructive of these ends, it is the Right of the People to alter or to abolish it, and to institute new Government, laying its foundation on such principles and organizing its powers in such form, as to them shall seem most likely to effect their Safety and Happiness. Prudence, indeed, will dictate that Governments long established should not be changed for light and transient causes; and accordingly all experience hath shewn, that mankind are more disposed to suffer, while evils are sufferable, than to right themselves by abolishing the forms to which they are accustomed. But when a long train of abuses and usurpations, pursuing invariably the same Object evinces a design to reduce them under absolute Despotism, it is their right, it is their duty, to throw off such Government, and to provide new Guards for their future security—Such has been the patient sufferance of these Colonies; and such is now the necessity which constrains them to alter their former Systems of Government. The history of the present King of Great Britain is a history of repeated injuries and usurpations, all having in direct object the establishment of an absolute Tyranny over these States. To provide this, let Facts be submitted to a candid world.

Grievances Against the King of England

He has refused his Assent to Laws, the most wholesome and necessary for the public good.

He has forbidden his Governors to pass Laws of immediate and pressing importance, unless suspended in their operation till his Assent should be obtained; and when so suspended, he has utterly neglected to attend to them.

He has refused to pass other Laws for the accommodation of large districts of people, unless those people would relinquish the right of Representation in the Legislature, a right inestimable to them and formidable to tyrants only.

He has called together legislative bodies at places unusual, uncomfortable, and distant from the depository of their public Records, for the sole purpose of fatiguing them into compliance with his measures.

He has dissolved Representative Houses repeatedly, for opposing with manly firmness his invasions on the rights of the people.

He has refused for a long time, after such dissolutions, to cause others to be elected; whereby the Legislative powers, incapable of Annihilation, have returned to the People at large for their exercise; the State remaining in the mean time exposed to all the dangers of invasion from without, and convulsions within.

He has endeavoured to prevent the population of these States; for that purpose obstructing the Laws for Naturalization of Foreigners; refusing to pass others to encourage their migrations hither, and raising the conditions of new Appropriations of Lands.

He has obstructed the Administration of Justice, by refusing his Assent to Laws for establishing Judiciary powers.

He has made Judges dependent on his Will alone, for the tenure of their offices, and the amount and payment of their salaries.

He has erected a multitude of New Offices, and sent hither swarms of Officers to harass our people, and eat out their substance.

He has kept among us, in times of peace, Standing Armies without the Consent of our legislatures.

He has affected to render the Military independent of and superior to the Civil power.

He has combined with others to subject us to a jurisdiction foreign to our constitution, and unacknowledged by our laws; giving his Assent to their Acts of pretended Legislation:

For Quartering large bodies of armed troops among us:

For protecting them, by a mock Trial, from punishment for any Murders which they should commit on the Inhabitants of these States:

For cutting off our Trade with all parts of the world:

For imposing Taxes on us without our Consent:

For depriving us in many cases, of the benefits of Trial by Jury:

For transporting us beyond Seas to be tried for pretended offences:

For abolishing the free System of English Laws in a neighbouring Province, establishing therein an Arbitrary government, and enlarging its Boundaries so as to render it at once an example and fit instrument for introducing the same absolute rule into these Colonies:

For taking away our Charters, abolishing our most valuable Laws, and altering fundamentally the Forms of our Governments:

For suspending our own Legislatures, and declaring themselves invested with power to legislate for us in all cases whatsoever.

He has abdicated Government here, by declaring us out of his Protection and waging War against us.

He has plundered our seas, ravaged our Coasts, burnt our towns, and destroyed the lives of our people.

He is at this time transporting large Armies of foreign Mercenaries to compleat the works of death, desolation and tyranny, already begun with circumstances of Cruelty & perfidy scarcely paralleled in the most barbarous ages, and totally unworthy the Head of a civilized nation.

He has constrained our fellow Citizens taken Captive on the high Seas to bear Arms against their Country, to become the executioners of their friends and Brethren, or to fall themselves by their Hands.

He has excited domestic insurrections amongst us, and has endeavoured to bring on the inhabitants of our frontiers, the merciless Indian Savages whose known rule of warfare, is an undistinguished destruction of all ages, sexes and conditions.

The States Will Be Free

In every stage of these Oppressions We have Petitioned for Redress in the most humble terms: Our repeated Petitions have been answered only by repeated injury. A Prince whose character is thus marked by every act which may define a Tyrant, is unfit to be the ruler of a free people.

Nor have We been wanting in attentions to our British brethren. We have warned them from time to time of attempts by their legislature to extend an unwarrantable jurisdiction over us. We have reminded them of the circumstances of our emigration and settlement here. We have appealed to their native justice and magnanimity, and we have conjured them by the ties of our common kindred to disavow these usurpations, which, would inevitably interrupt our connections and correspondence. They too have been deaf to the voice of justice and of consanguinity. We must, therefore, acquiesce in the necessity, which denounces our Separation, and hold them, as we hold the rest of mankind, Enemies in War, in Peace Friends.

We, therefore, the Representatives of the united States of America, in General Congress, Assembled, appealing to the Supreme Judge of the world for the rectitude of our intentions, do, in the Name, and by Authority of the good People of these Colonies, solemnly publish and declare, That these United Colonies are, and of Right ought to be Free and Independent States; that they are Absolved from all Allegiance to the British Crown, and that all political connection between them and the State of Great Britain, is and ought to be totally dissolved; and that as Free and Independent States, they have full Power to levy War, conclude Peace, contract Alliances, establish Commerce, and to do all other Acts and Things which Independent States may of right do. And for the support of this Declaration, with a firm reliance on the protection of divine Providence, we mutually pledge to each other our Lives, our Fortunes and our sacred Honor.

Democracy Has Affected the Social Condition of Americans

Alexis de Tocqueville

When Alexis de Tocqueville, a French political thinker and histo-rian, visited the United States in the 1830s he found a flourish-ing democracy not seen anywhere else in the world. In his two-volume Democracy in America, *published in 1835, de Tocqueville offers insightful observations on American society and its political institutions. In the chapter reproduced here, he examines why the early American colonists became more and more democratic. He says that the changes in the laws regarding inheritance of private property among the settlers resulted in the more rapid division of land and forced people to seek wealth outside of the family estate to maintain their previous standard of living. This, he argues, accelerated the death of the landed ar-istocracy and hastened the move to democracy.*

A social condition is commonly the result of circumstances, sometimes of laws, oftener still of these two causes united; but wherever it exists, it may justly be considered as the source of almost all the laws, the usages, and the ideas which regulate the conduct of nations; whatever it does not produce it modifies. It is therefore necessary, if we would be-come acquainted with the legislation and the manners of a nation, to begin by the study of its social condition.

The Social Condition of the Anglo-Americans Is Its Essential Democracy

Many important observations suggest themselves upon the so-cial condition of the Anglo-Americans, but there is one which takes precedence of all the rest. The social condition of the

Alexis de Tocqueville, "Social Condition of the Anglo-Americans," *Democracy in America*, translated by Henry Reeve, New York: The Colonial Press, 1899, pp. 46–54.

Americans is eminently democratic; this was its character at the foundation of the Colonies, and is still more strongly marked at the present day. . . .

Great equality existed among the emigrants who settled on the shores of New England. The germ of aristocracy was never planted in that part of the Union. The only influence which obtained there was that of intellect; the people were used to reverence certain names as the emblems of knowledge and virtue. Some of their fellow-citizens acquired a power over the rest which might truly have been called aristocratic, if it had been capable of transmission from father to son.

This was the state of things to the east of the Hudson [river running north and south in the eastern portion of New York State]: to the south-west of that river, and in the direction of the Floridas, the case was different. In most of the States situated to the south-west of the Hudson some great English proprietors had settled, who had imported with them aristocratic principles and the English law of descent. . . . In the South, one man, aided by slaves, could cultivate a great extent of country: it was therefore common to see rich landed proprietors. But their influence was not altogether aristocratic as that term is understood in Europe, since they possessed no privileges; and the cultivation of their estates being carried on by slaves, they had no tenants depending on them, and consequently no patronage. Still, the great proprietors south of the Hudson constituted a superior class, having ideas and tastes of its own, and forming the centre of political action. This kind of aristocracy sympathized with the body of the people, whose passions and interests it easily embraced; but it was too weak and too short-lived to excite either love or hatred for itself. This was the class which headed the insurrection in the South, and furnished the best leaders of the American revolution.

New Laws for a New People

At the period of which we are now speaking society was shaken to its centre: the people, in whose name the struggle had taken place, conceived the desire of exercising the authority which it had acquired; its democratic tendencies were awakened; and having thrown off the yoke of the mother-country, it aspired to independence, of every kind. The influence of individuals gradually ceased to be felt, and custom and law united together to produce the same result.

But the law of descent was the last step to equality. I am surprised that ancient and modern jurists have not attributed to this law a greater influence on human affairs. It is true that these laws belong to civil affairs; but they ought nevertheless to be placed at the head of all political institutions; for, whilst political laws are only the symbol of a nation's condition, they exercise an incredible influence upon its social state. They have, moreover, a sure and uniform manner of operating upon society, affecting, as it were, generations yet unborn.

Through their means man acquires a kind of preternatural power over the future lot of his fellow-creatures. When the legislator has regulated the law of inheritance, he may rest from his labor. The machine once put in motion will go on for ages, and advance, as if self-guided, towards a given point. When framed in a particular manner, this law unites, draws together, and vests property and power in a few hands: its tendency is clearly aristocratic. On opposite principles its action is still more rapid; it divides, distributes, and disperses both property and power. Alarmed by the rapidity of its progress, those who despair of arresting its motion endeavor to obstruct it by difficulties and impediments; they vainly seek to counteract its effect by contrary efforts; but it gradually reduces or destroys every obstacle, until by its incessant activity the bulwarks of the influence of wealth are ground down to the fine and shifting sand which is the basis of democracy. When the law of inheritance permits, still more when it decrees, the equal division of a father's property amongst all his children, its effects are of two kinds: it is important to distinguish them from each other, although they tend to the same end.

In virtue of the law of partible inheritance, the death of every proprietor brings about a kind of revolution in property; not only do his possessions change hands, but their very nature is altered, since they are parceled into shares, which become smaller and smaller at each division. This is the direct and, as it were, the physical effect of the law. It follows, then, that in countries where equality of inheritance is established by law, property, and especially landed property, must have a tendency to perpetual diminution [reduction]. The effects, however, of, such legislation would only be perceptible after a lapse of time, if the law was abandoned to its own working; for supposing the family to consist of two children (and in a country peopled as France the average number is not above three), these children, sharing amongst them the fortune of both parents, would not be poorer than their father or mother.

But the law of equal division exercises its influence not merely upon the property itself, but it affects the minds of the heirs, and brings their passions into play. These indirect consequences tend powerfully to the destruction of large fortunes, and especially of large domains. Among nations whose law of descent is founded upon the right of primogeniture [the right of the eldest child—most often the eldest son—to inherit the entire estate of one or both parents], landed estates often pass from generation to generation without undergoing division, the consequences of which is that family feeling is to a certain degree incorporated with the state. The family represents the state, the state the family; whose name, together with its origin, its glory, its power, and its virtues, is thus perpetuated in an imperishable memorial of the past and a sure pledge of the future.

When the equal partition of property is established by law, the intimate connection is destroyed between family feeling and the preservation of the paternal estate; the property ceases to represent the family; for as it must inevitably be divided after one or two generations, it has evidently a constant tendency to diminish, and must in the end be completely dispersed. The sons of the great landed proprietor, if they are few in number, or if fortune befriends them, may indeed entertain the hope of being as wealthy as their father, but not that of possessing the same property as he did; the riches must necessarily be composed of elements different from his.

Now, from the moment that you divest the landowner of that interest in the preservation of his estate which he derives from association, from tradition, and from family pride, you may be certain that sooner or later he will dispose of it; for there is a strong pecuniary interest in favor of selling, as floating capital produces higher interest than real property, and is more readily available to gratify the passions of the moment.

Great landed estates which have once been divided never come together again; for the small proprietor draws from his land a better revenue, in proportion, than the large owner does from his, and of course he sells it at a higher rate. The calculations of gain, therefore, which decide the rich man to sell his domain will still more powerfully influence him against buying small estates to unite them into a large one.

What is called family pride is often founded upon an illusion of self-love. A man wishes to perpetuate and immortalize himself, as it were, in his great-grandchildren. Where the *esprit de famille* [family pride] ceases to act, individual selfishness comes into play. When the idea of family becomes vague, indeterminate and uncertain, a man thinks of his present convenience; he provides for the establishment of his succeeding generation, and no more. Either a man gives up the idea of perpetuating his family, or at any rate he seeks to accomplish it by other means than that of a landed estate.

Thus not only does the law of partible inheritance render it difficult for families to preserve their ancestral domains entire, but it deprives them of the inclination to attempt it, and compels them in some measure to co-operate with the law in their own extinction.

The law of equal distribution proceeds by two methods: by acting upon things, it acts upon persons; by influencing persons, it affects things. By these means the law succeeds in striking at the root of landed property, and dispersing rapidly both families and fortunes.

Most certainly it is not for us Frenchmen of the nineteenth century, who daily witness the political and social changes which the law of partition is bringing to pass, to question its influence. It is perpetually conspicuous in our country, overthrowing the walls of our dwellings and removing the landmarks of our fields. But although it has produced great effects in France, much still remains for it to do. Our recollections, opinions, and habits present powerful obstacles to its progress.

In the United States it has nearly completed its work of destruction, and there we can best study its results. The English laws concerning the transmission of property were abolished in almost all the States at the time of the Revolution. The law of entail was so modified as not to interrupt the free circulation of property. The first generation having passed away, estates began to be parcelled out, and the change became more and more rapid with the progress of time. At this moment, after a lapse of a little more than sixty years, the aspect of society the families of the great landed proprietors are almost all commingled with the general mass. In the State of New York, which formerly contained many of these, there are but two who still keep their heads above the stream, and they must shortly disappear. The sons of these opulent citizens are become merchants, lawyers, or physicians. Most of them have lapsed into obscurity. The last trace of hereditary ranks and distinctions is destroyed—the law of partition has reduced all to one level.

Wealth Is No Longer Inheritance

I do not mean that there is any deficiency of wealthy individuals in the United States; I know of no country, indeed, where the love of money has taken stronger hold on the affections of men, and where the profounder contempt is expressed for the theory of the permanent equality of property. But wealth circulates with inconceivable rapidity, and experience shows that it is rare to find two succeeding generations in the full enjoyment of it.

This picture, which may perhaps be thought to be overcharged, still gives a very imperfect idea of what is taking place in the new States of the West and South-west. At the end of the last century a few bold adventurers began to penetrate into the valleys of the Mississippi, and the mass of the population very soon began to move in that direction: communities unheard of till then were seen to emerge from the wilds: States whose names were not in existence a few years before claimed their place in the American Union; and in the Western settlements we may behold democracy arrived at its utmost extreme. In these States, founded off-hand, and, as it were, by chance, the inhabitants are but of yesterday. Scarcely known to one another, the nearest neighbors are ignorant of each other's history. In this part of the American continent, therefore, the population has not experienced the influence of great names and great wealth, nor even that of the natural aristocracy of knowledge and virtue. None are there to wield that respectable power which men willingly grant to the remembrance of a life spent in doing good before their eyes. The new States of the West are already inhabited, but society has no existence among them.

It is not only the fortunes of men which are equal in America; even their requirements partake in some degree of the same uniformity. I do not believe that there is a country in the world where, in proportion to the population, there are so few uninstructed and at the same time so few learned individuals. Primary instruction is within the reach of everybody; superior instruction is scarcely to be obtained by any. This is not surprising; it is in fact the necessary consequence of what we have advanced above. Almost all the Americans are in easy circumstances, and can therefore obtain the first elements of human knowledge.

In America there are comparatively few who are rich enough to live without a profession. Every profession requires an apprenticeship, which limits the time of instruction to the early years of life. At fifteen they enter upon their calling, and thus their education ends at the age when ours begins. Whatever is done afterwards is with a view to some special and lucrative object; a science is taken up as a matter of business, and the only branch of it which is attended to is such as admits of an immediate practical application. In America most of the rich men were formerly poor; most of those who now enjoy leisure were absorbed in business during their youth; the consequence of which is, that when they might have had a taste for study they had no time for it, and when time is at their disposal they have no longer the inclination.

There is no class, then, in America, in which the taste for intellectual pleasures is transmitted with hereditary fortune and leisure, and by which the labors of the intellect are held in honor. Accordingly there is an equal want of the desire and the power of application to these objects.

A middle standard is fixed in America for human knowledge. All approach as near to it as they can; some as they rise, others as they descend. Of course, an immense multitude of persons are to be found who entertain the same number of ideas on religion, history, science, political economy, legislation, and government. The gifts of intellect proceed directly from God, and man cannot prevent their unequal distribution. But in consequence of the state of things which we have here represented it happens that, although the capacities of men are widely different, as the Creator has doubtless intended they should be, they are submitted to the same method of treatment.

In America the aristocratic element has always been feeble from its birth; and if at the present day it is not actually destroyed, it is at any rate so completely disabled that we can scarcely assign to it any degree of influence in the course of affairs. The democratic principle, on the contrary, has gained so much strength by time, by events, and by legislation, as to have become not only predominant but all-powerful. There is no family or corporate authority, and it is rare to find even the influence of individual character enjoy any durability.

America, then, exhibits in her social state a most extraordinary phenomenon. Men are there seen on a greater equality in point of fortune and intellect, or, in other words, more equal in their strength, than in any other country of the world, or in any age of which history has preserved the remembrance.

Political Consequences

The political consequences of such a social condition as this are easily deducible. It is impossible to believe that equality will not eventually find its way into the political world as it does everywhere else. To conceive of men remaining forever unequal upon one single point, yet equal on all others, is impossible; they must come in the end to be equal upon all. Now I know of only two methods of establishing equality in the political world; every citizen must be put in possession of his rights, or rights must be granted to no one. For nations which are arrived at the same stage of social existence as the Anglo-Americans, it is therefore very difficult to discover a medium between the sovereignty of all and the absolute power of one man: and it would be vain to deny that the social condition which I have been describing is equally liable to each of these consequences.

There is, in fact, a manly and lawful passion for equality which excites men to wish all to be powerful and honored. This passion tends to elevate the humble to the rank of the great; but there exists also in the human heart a depraved taste for equality, which impels the weak to attempt to lower the powerful to their own level, and reduces men to prefer equality in slavery to inequality with freedom. Not that those nations whose social condition is democratic naturally despise liberty; on the contrary, they have an instinctive love of it. But liberty is not the chief and constant object of their desires; equality is their idol: they make rapid and sudden efforts to obtain liberty, and if they miss their aim resign themselves to their disappointment; but nothing can satisfy them except equality, and rather than lose it they resolve to perish.

On the other hand, in a State where the citizens are nearly on an equality, it becomes difficult for them to preserve their independence against the aggressions of power. No one among them being strong enough to engage in the struggle with advantage, nothing but a general combination can protect their liberty. And such a union is not always to be found.

From the same social position, then, nations may derive one or the other of two great political results; these results are extremely different from each other, but they may both proceed from the same cause.

The Anglo-Americans are the first nations who, having been exposed to this formidable alternative, have been happy enough to escape the dominion of absolute power. They have been allowed by their circumstances, their origin, their intelligence, and especially by their moral feeling, to establish and maintain the sovereignty of the people.

A Nation Conceived in Liberty

Abraham Lincoln

Few documents in the growth of American democracy are as well known as the short speech President Abraham Lincoln delivered at the dedication of the military cemetery in Gettysburg, Pennsylvania, in 1863. The Battle of Gettysburg was the turning point in the Civil War, and Lincoln's presence at the dedication of the battlefield and cemetery provided him an opportunity for a major speech. He spoke for only two minutes, uttering a mere 266 words, but Lincoln's famous address transformed the meaning of the U.S. Constitution. In his speech, Lincoln reads into the Constitution a promise of equality, the "proposition that all men are created equal." Equality had been a premise of the Declaration of Independence, but it was generally understood that the drafters of that document had not intended to include slaves and other "inferior" peoples in their definition. Lincoln proclaims that the lives of the men who fought at Gettysburg and in the entire war would not be in vain only if the nation, finally, lived up to the proposition that all of its people, regardless of race, were in fact equal. The power of Lincoln's idea still informs American democratic thought.

Fourscore and seven years ago our fathers brought forth on this continent a new nation, conceived in liberty, and dedicated to the proposition that all men are created equal.

Now we are engaged in a great war, testing whether that nation, or any nation so conceived and so dedicated, can long endure. We are met on a great battlefield of that war. We have come to dedicate a portion of that field as a final resting-place for those who here gave their lives that this nation might live. It is altogether fitting and proper that we should do this.

But, in a larger sense, we cannot dedicate . . . we cannot consecrate . . . we cannot hallow . . . this ground. The brave

Abraham Lincoln, the Gettysburg Address, November 19, 1863.

men, living and dead, who struggled here, have consecrated it far above our power to add or detract. The world will little note nor long remember what we say here, but it can never forget what they did here. It is for us, the living, rather to be dedicated here to the unfinished work which they who fought here have thus far so nobly advanced. It is rather for us to be here dedicated to the great task remaining before us ... that from these honored dead we take increased devotion to the cause for which they gave the last full measure of devotion; that we here highly resolve that these dead shall not have died in vain; that this nation, under God, shall have a new birth of freedom; and that government of the people, by the people, for the people, shall not perish from the earth.

November 19, 1863

An Appeal for Equal Rights

Langston Hughes

The African American poet, novelist, playwright, and short-fiction writer Langston Hughes was one of the great minds of the early twentieth century and a leading figure in the Harlem Renaissance movement. His highly political works promoted equality, condemned racism and injustice, and celebrated African American culture and identity. Many of his poems offer twin themes of protest and hope, showing how while America was a country in which the seeds of democracy had been sowed and the ideal of democracy nurtured, its dream was not yet fulfilled. In "Dear Mr. President," Hughes urges President Franklin D. Roosevelt to consider the plight of the black man who, having fought for his country, must return to a segregated, unequal society.

Dear Mr. President
President Roosevelt, you
Are our Commander in Chief.
As such, I appeal
To you for relief.
Respectfully, sir,
I await your reply
As I train here to fight,
Perhaps to die.
I am a soldier
Down in Alabam
Wearing the uniform
Of Uncle Sam.
But when I get on the bus

I have to ride in the back.
Rear seats only
For a man who's black.
When I get on the train,
It's the Jim Crow car—
That don't seem to jibe
With what we're fighting for.
Mr. President, sir,
I don't understand
Democracy that
Forgets the black man.
Respectfully, therefore,
I call your attention
To these Jim Crow laws
Your speeches don't mention.
I ask why YOUR soldiers
Must ride in the back,
Segregated—
Because we are black?
I train to fight,
Perhaps to die.
Urgently, sir,
I await your reply.

Advances in American Democracy Have Been Reversed by Current Policy

Mark Green

Mark Green, the former public advocate for New York City, is president of the New Democracy Project and author of Losing Our Democracy. *In the following article, he argues that President George W. Bush has seriously undermined American democracy with the authoritarian actions of his legislative branch. Green also believes that Bush and his supporters—in the clergy, in large corporations, and in Congress—have threatened constitutional traditions that now need to be rescued. He explains that the Democracy Protection Act developed by Green's New Democracy Project and others can help the United States recover from what he regards as Bush's assaults and fix the flaws created by Bush that have diminished American democracy and frustrated majority support for progressive reforms. The act, he points out, identifies five key areas calling out for popular reform.*

> Democracy can come undone. It's not something that's necessarily going to last forever once it's been established.
> —Sean Wilentz, *The Rise of American Democracy*

Now that the Democrats' "100 hours agenda" [a list of promises made by House Democrats to be initiated in the first one hundred hours of the 110th Congress, beginning January 3, 2007] has at least passed the House—and as [George W.] Bush & Co. head toward retirement—the hard work of restoring our democracy must begin. For while the President frequently talks about exporting democracy, he has systematically undermined it here at home.

Mark Green, "How to Fix Our Democracy," *The Nation*, February 28, 2007. www.thenation.com. Reproduced by permission.

Not that this democracy was perfect before Bush had his way with it. If democracy means majority rule, minority rights and the rule of law, then the Constitution contained language that was far from democratic. Only men with property could vote. Blacks counted as three-fifths of a person. The Senate was not elected, and states of varying sizes had the same representation.

Yet despite this flawed start, our system evolved into a stronger democracy. Senators became popularly elected in 1913; women won the vote in 1920 and African-Americans forty-five years later. In the 1930s, '60s and '90s, Democratic administrations showed that a democracy could expand public healthcare, provide for old-age insurance, make products safer and clean the air.

This two-century advance has recently been reversed. A powerful group of new authoritarians in the executive branch, Congress, the clergy and corporations have expressed enormous contempt for the conversation of democracy. Trampling on the values represented by the flag far more than the couple of fools a year who actually burn one, these leaders pose a clear and present danger to our constitutional traditions. This quiet crisis of democracy—lacking the vivid imagery of a Hindenburg [zeppelin disaster of 1937], a 9/11 [September 11, 2001, terrorist attacks on America] or soldiers being shot in Iraq—has attracted very little attention. But a better democracy requires better policies. With the Democrats finally back on the offensive, it's time to repair the broken machinery of government.

The Democracy Protection Act—developed by the New Democracy Project, the Brennan Center for Justice, Demos [Democrats] and *The Nation*—can help us recover from Bush's assaults as well as fix structural flaws that have long diminished our democracy and frustrated majority support for progressive reforms. It identifies five key areas calling out for popular reform.

Taking Liberties with the Law

Apparently, when Bush swore to "faithfully execute the laws," he took that oath literally. In just six years, his Administration has, in violation of the UN [United Nations] Charter, invaded a country, condoned torture, refused to seek warrants for wiretaps, leaked classified information for partisan gain, rounded up thousands of American Muslims without evidence, incarcerated hundreds at Guantánamo [U.S. Navy detention camp] without charges, restricted habeas corpus [a writ protecting against illegal imprisonment] and asserted the power to ignore hundreds of duly enacted laws—all because of an open-ended "war on terror."

For 200 years after *Marbury v. Madison* courts had the final say on interpreting laws and the Constitution. Then Bush aides forwarded the "unitary executive" theory, according to which the President may nullify laws after signing them. He has produced 800 "signing statements" so far, asserting that if he thinks a law unwise, he simply won't enforce it—*Marbury* be damned.

When Bush, defending his flagrant violation of the 1978 Foreign Intelligence Surveillance Act, argued that the requirement of warrants for wiretaps could be ignored because of his "inherent powers" in wartime, it was too much even for a veteran of President [Ronald] Reagan's Justice Department. "This is a defining moment in the constitutional history of the United States," said [constitutional law attorney] Bruce Fein. "The theory invoked by the president . . . would equally justify mail openings, burglaries, torture or internment camps, all in the name of gathering foreign intelligence."

It took the Supreme Court—seven of whose nine members were appointed by conservative Republican Presidents—to remind Bush in both the 2004 *Hamdi* [Supreme Court decision that affirmed the due process rights of U.S. citizens deemed "enemy combatants"] and 2006 *Hamdan* [Supreme Court decision declaring that the trial commissions of detainees at Guantánamo violate military and international law] decisions that the rule of law is not a means but an end in itself. "A state of war," wrote Justice Sandra Day O'Connor in *Hamdi*, "is not a blank check for the President."

The Legislative Broken Branch

Under the recent [Tom] DeLay/[Dennis] Hastert Congressional regime, Democrats were cut out of bill-writing while corporate lobbyists sat with [Capitol] Hill staff drafting legislation. Congress abdicated its checks-and-balances function entirely, becoming little more than a West Wing of the White House. The House held 140 hours of hearings, for example, into whether President [Bill] Clinton used his Christmas list for fundraising and twelve into abuses at Abu Ghraib [prison camp in Iraq where U.S. military officers were found guilty of abusing and torturing detainees]. Speaker Dennis Hastert would only schedule a bill for a vote if it had support from a "majority of the majority" party and would hold a vote open for as many hours as necessary to secure—i.e., arm-twist—a victory. Senator Hillary Clinton was right to call that system "a plantation."

But the crisis of democracy in our legislative branch has hardly abated just because the GOP [Grand Old Party, nickname of the Republican Party] was trounced in November [2006]. Money rather than merit so often determines elections that Congressional incumbents listen more to donors than to voters. Accountability has been further eroded by politicized redistricting, which means fewer and fewer competitive elections. The defeat of twenty incumbent House Republicans (it was five in 2002 and four in 2004) is not serious evidence to the contrary: A twelve-point polling spread favoring Republicans in 1994 led to a fifty-two-seat switch that year, while a larger, fifteen-point gap favoring Democrats produced only a thirty-seat switch in 2006.

There is also a stunning violation of democracy built into the Senate that should be part of any discussion about majority rule. Today California, with a population of 36 million, elects 2 percent of the Senate, while twenty-one other states with the same total population elect 42 percent. It's surely not "one person, one vote" when people living in the smallest states have twenty times the say as people in the largest. The Electoral College is similarly biased toward small, rural, largely red [heavily Republican] states—something to recall next time a conservative politician rails against a judicial filibuster or affirmative action.

A Democracy Without Voters

By the gauge of electoral turnout, America is in the bottom fifth of democracies in the world. Compare our recent average turnout of 48 percent of eligible voters in presidential years to Cambodia's 90 percent, Western Europe's 77 percent and Eastern Europe's 68 percent. If there were a World Bank index of "democracy poverty," the United States would be a candidate for massive international aid.

In most states, cumbersome rules discourage the vote. Why should voter registration laws presume that thousands of 18-year-olds each find their way to an Election Board, instead of having one Election Board representative go to each high school?

In addition, local political operatives often suppress the vote in discriminatory ways, as we witnessed in Ohio in 2004. Beyond the well-known example of Republican officials intentionally failing to provide sufficient voting machines in low-income Democratic precincts, conservative activists also put up signs in African-American areas of Cuyahoga County [Ohio] telling voters that if anyone in their family voted illegally they could lose custody of their children, that they couldn't vote if they had unpaid utility bills and that Republicans were supposed to vote on Tuesday and Democrats on

Wednesday! The intent of these and other crass intimidation tactics was plainly revealed in 2004 by Representative John Pappageorge, a Michigan Republican, when he said, "If we do not suppress the Detroit vote [a heavily African American, low-income community] we're going to have a tough time in this election cycle."

One way most states, especially in the Old South, suppress the low-income vote legally is through felony disenfranchisement laws. Even though they've "paid their debt to society," ex-cons in thirty-five states are deprived of the right to vote, which means, for example, that one in six black men in Alabama is excluded. Seven million Americans—or one in thirty-two—are currently behind bars, on parole or on probation, and they are disproportionately African-American and Latino. Felony disenfranchisement laws are just another way to spell Jim Crow [laws that granted separate but equal status to blacks].

Nor has the controversy over counting votes ended with those chads in Florida [tabs not completely punched through on paper ballots that affected the 2000 presidential election]. While the 2002 Help America Vote Act properly required that states move to electronic voting (something Brazil figured out how to do a decade ago), many of the electronic machines used last November [2006] provided no paper trail, a failure whose repercussions are now on view in the continuing imbroglio over the Sarasota, Florida, Congressional seat. And as the Brennan Center for Justice has documented, most electronic machines are easily hackable. Will we find out in twenty years that a handful of Republican operatives re-elected W. [Bush] by rigging some software in Ohio?

Secrecy and Democracy

Remember that early aphorism of the computer age, "Garbage in, garbage out"? Just as machines fail when fed corrupt information, democracy fails when important decisions are based on bad data or no data.

The good people of Salem, Massachusetts, were sure that certain women were possessed, and many Americans were convinced of the need to invade Iraq because George W. Bush downplayed the risks and hinted that Saddam [Hussein] played a role in 9/11. When ideology trumps facts, the results are often disastrous.

To insure a healthy democracy with plenty of well-reasoned debate, then, secrets should be kept to a minimum. Yet during the hot and cold wars of the twentieth century, as the late Senator Daniel Patrick Moynihan pointed out, a "culture of secrecy" took root in Washington. And the Bush Administration has deepened this culture, skillfully capitalizing on the calamity of 9/11 to hide information in the name of "national security" and concentrate authority in the "war President." Patrick Leahy, chair of the Senate Judiciary Committee, says, "Of the six administrations I've worked with, this is the most secretive."

The Economics of Democracy

Economist Jeff Madrick, writing in 2003, asked some difficult questions as part of a lengthy analysis of the US economy: "Where does income and wealth inequality start to impinge on civil and political rights and on America's long commitment to equality of economic opportunity? Where does it both reflect a failure of democracy and contribute to its weakening?" When the head of ExxonMobil recently earned $368 million in a year—more *per hour* than his workers earn *per year*—it's not hard to see why Madrick concluded, "There is a good argument to be made that we are already there." The rich have become the super-rich, and middle-class families feel as if they're running up a down escalator. Even a snapshot of the data is convincing: In 1980 the wealthiest 5 percent of US households earned 16.5 percent of all income; in 1990 it was 18.5 percent; in 2000, 22.1 percent. Meanwhile, real median income for men has fallen for five straight years. The number of poor has increased from 31 million to 37 million since 2000, and the number without health insurance rose from 41 million to 47 million.

Not since the Gilded Age, when wealthy businessmen effectively appointed senators, has big business held such sway in Washington. Scores of laws and policies implemented by Bush 43—cutting job-training programs, eroding the minimum wage, slashing taxes on the rich and social programs for the poor—have hastened the tilt from labor to capital. George Bush has redistributed wealth far more than [former South Dakota senator and 1972 Democratic presidential candidate] George McGovern was ever accused of—except up, not down.

Or as [former Supreme Court justice] Louis Brandeis wrote: "We can have democracy in this country, or we can have great wealth concentrated in the hands of a few, but we can't have both."

Emergencies are easy ways to justify extremism, as radicals from Father [Charles] Coughlin [politically radical Catholic priest who gave radio talks in the 1930s] to Joe McCarthy [U.S. senator who sought out Communists in America] have taught us. But today America is witnessing an authoritarian impulse from those at the highest levels of government.

When questioned two years ago about his failed policy in Iraq, Bush famously said, "We had an accountability moment and that's called the 2004 elections," casually dismissing the checks and balances built into our government for the 1,460 days between presidential elections. Last fall, former Speaker Newt Gingrich suggested that we suspend parts of the First Amendment during the "war on terrorism." In January White House press secretary Tony Snow said the President "has the ability to exercise his own authority if he thinks Congress has voted the wrong way." And now Bush and [Vice President Dick] Cheney are implying that they can attack Iran at will, without any prior Congressional authorization, in clear violation of the Constitution and statutory law. We are edging toward what James Madison warned of [in *Marbury vs. Madison*], in a line cited in the *Hamdan* decision: "The accumulation of all powers legislative, executive and judiciary, in the same hands, whether of one, a few or many, and whether hereditary, self-appointed or elective, may justly be pronounced the very definition of tyranny."

So just as the last half of the twentieth century saw a quadrupling of the number of democracies around the globe—just as, in the view of historian John Lewis Gaddis, "the world came closer than ever before to reaching a consensus . . . that only democracy confers legitimacy"—the world's oldest democracy is being systematically undermined by radical reactionaries. We are another Bush/Cheney White House, another DeLay Congress, another [Antonin] Scalia on the [Supreme] Court away from permanently losing our democracy. In six short years, George W. Bush has not only blown a large inherited federal surplus, he has also squandered an inheritance of centuries of democracy progress. That's not alarmist. It's merely descriptive of the quiet crisis our democracy now faces.

At a December [2006] colloquium on this subject in New York City, [journalist] Bill Moyers observed that what America needs is not just a "must do" list from liberals but "a different story," one with the power to inspire us and challenge the prevailing conservative narrative of private = good, public = bad. That story is democracy. While theocrats and plutocrats pose as populists, it's essential that progressive patriots—for what can be more patriotic than democracy?—erect stronger levees to withstand the oceans of money, lobbyists and lawless officials threatening to drown America's constitutional traditions. For only then can our government represent the large majorities in favor of universal healthcare, stricter gun control, withdrawal from Iraq and more.

The Democracy Protection Act is offered up to officials, activists and citizens alike in the spirit of [poet] Walt Whitman, who wrote that "America is always becoming."

The United States Falls Short of True Democracy

Noam Chomsky

Noam Chomsky, a former professor of linguistics at the Massachusetts Institute of Technology, has been called "arguably the most important living intellectual in the United States." In the following interview with Daniel Mermet, Chomsky explains that White House policy does not reflect the will of the majority, and thus the United States is not a true democracy. He further illustrates his view of the country's shortcomings, and provides his theory of the role of the state in a democratic nation.

Daniel Mermet: Let's start with the media issue. In the May 2005 referendum on the European constitution, most newspapers in France supported a yes vote, yet 55% of the electorate voted no. This suggests there is a limit to how far the media can manipulate public opinion. Do you think voters were also saying no to the media?

Noam Chomsky: It's a complex subject, but the little in-depth research carried out in this field suggests that, in fact, the media exert greater influence over the most highly educated fraction of the population. Mass public opinion seems less influenced by the line adopted by the media.

Take the eventuality of a war against Iran. Three-quarters of Americans think the United States should stop its military threats and concentrate on reaching agreement by diplomatic means. Surveys carried out by western pollsters suggest that public opinion in Iran and the US is also moving closer on some aspects of the nuclear issue. The vast majority of the population of both countries think that the area from Israel to

Iran should be completely clear of nuclear weapons, including those held by US forces operating in the region. But you would have to search long and hard to find this kind of information in the media.

The main political parties in either country do not defend this view either. If Iran and the US were true democracies, in which the majority really decided public policy, they would undoubtedly have already solved the current nuclear disagreement. And there are other similar instances. Look at the US federal budget. Most Americans want less military spending and more welfare expenditure, credits for the United Nations [UN], and economic and international humanitarian aid. They also want to cancel the tax reductions decided by President George [W.] Bush for the benefit of the biggest taxpayers.

On all these topics, White House policy is completely at odds with what public opinion wants. But the media rarely publish the polls that highlight this persistent public opposition. Not only are citizens excluded from political power, they are also kept in a state of ignorance as to the true state of public opinion. There is growing international concern about the massive US double deficit affecting trade and the budget. But both are closely linked to a third deficit, the democratic deficit that is constantly growing, not only in the US but all over the western world.

When a leading journalist or TV news presenter is asked whether they are subject to pressure or censorship, they say they are completely free to express their own opinions. So how does thought control work in a democratic society? We know how it works in dictatorships.

As you say, journalists immediately reply: "No one has been exerting any pressure on me. I write what I want." And it's true. But if they defended positions contrary to the dominant norm, someone else would soon be writing editorials in their place. Obviously it is not a hard-and-fast rule: the US press sometimes publishes even my work, and the US is not a totalitarian country. But anyone who fails to fulfill certain minimum requirements does not stand a chance of becoming an established commentator.

It is one of the big differences between the propaganda system of a totalitarian state and the way democratic societies go about things. Exaggerating slightly, in totalitarian countries the state decides the official line and everyone must then comply. Democratic societies operate differently. The line is never presented as such, merely implied. This involves brainwashing people who are still at liberty. Even the passionate debates in the main media stay within the bounds of commonly accepted, implicit rules, which sideline a large number of contrary views. The system of control in democratic societies is extremely effective. We do not notice the line any more than we notice the air we breathe. We sometimes even imagine we are seeing a lively debate. The system of control is much more powerful than in totalitarian systems.

Look at Germany in the early 1930s. We tend to forget that it was the most advanced country in Europe, taking the lead in art, science, technology, literature and philosophy. Then, in no time at all, it suffered a complete reversal of fortune and became the most barbaric, murderous state in human history. All that was achieved by using fear: fear of the Bolsheviks, the Jews, the Americans, the Gypsies—everyone who, according to the Nazis, was threatening the core values of European culture and the direct descendants of Greek civilisation (as the philosopher Martin Heidegger wrote in 1935). However, most of the German media who inundated the population with these messages were using marketing techniques developed by US advertising agents.

The same method is always used to impose an ideology. Violence is not enough to dominate people: some other justification is required. When one person wields power over another—whether they are a dictator, a colonist, a bureaucrat, a spouse or a boss—they need an ideology justifying their action. And it is always the same: their domination is exerted for the good of the underdog. Those in power always present themselves as being altruistic, disinterested and generous.

In the 1930s the rules for Nazi propaganda involved using simple words and repeating them in association with emotions and phobia. When [Adolf] Hitler invaded the Sudetenland in 1938 he cited the noblest, most charitable motives: the need for a humanitarian intervention to prevent the ethnic cleansing of German speakers. Henceforward everyone would be living under Germany's protective wing, with the support of the world's most artistically and culturally advanced country.

When it comes to propaganda (though in a sense nothing has changed since the days of Athens) there have been some minor improvements. The instruments available now are much more refined, in partlcular—surprising as it may seem—in the countries with the greatest civil liberties, Britain and the US. The contemporary public relations industry was born there in the 1920s, an activity we may also refer to as opinion forming or propaganda.

Both countries had made such progress in democratic rights (women's suffrage, freedom of speech) that state violence was no longer sufficient to contain the desire for liberty. So those in power sought other ways of manufacturing consent. The PR [public relations] industry produces, in the true sense of the term, concept, acceptance and submission. It controls people's minds and ideas. It is a major advance on totalitarian rule, as it is much more agreeable to be subjected to advertising than to torture.

In the US, freedom of speech is protected to an extent that I think is unheard of in any other country. This is quite a recent change. Since the 1960s the Supreme Court has set very high standards for freedom of speech, in keeping with a basic principle established by the 18th century Enlightenment. The court upholds the principle of free speech, the only limitation being participation in a criminal act. If I walk into a shop to commit a robbery with an accomplice holding a gun and I say "Shoot," my words are not protected by the Constitution. Otherwise there has to be a really serious motive to call into question freedom of speech. The Supreme Court has even upheld this principle for the benefit of members of the Ku Klux Klan.

In France and Britain, and I believe the rest of Europe, the definition of freedom of speech is more restrictive. In my view the essential point is whether the state is entitled to determine historical truth and to punish those who contest such truth. If we allow the state to exert such powers we are accepting Stalinist methods [associated with the theory and practice of communism as devised by Joseph Stalin]. French intellectuals have difficulty admitting that they are inclined to do just that. Yet when we refuse such behaviour there should be no exceptions. The state should have no means of punishing anyone who claims that the sun rotates around the earth. There is a very elementary side to the principle of freedom of speech: either we defend it in the case of opinions we find hateful, or we do not defend it at all. Even Hitler and Stalin acknowledged the right to freedom of speech of those who were defending their point of view.

I find it distressing to have to discuss such issues two centuries after [the French philosopher] Voltaire who, as we all know, said: "I shall defend my opinions till I die, but I will give up my life so that you may defend yours." It would be a great disservice to the memory of the victims of the Holocaust to adopt one of the basic doctrines of their murderers.

In one of your books you quote [economist] Milton Friedman as saying that "profit-making is the essence of democracy."

Profit and democracy are so contrary that there is no scope for comment. The aim of democracy is to leave people free to decide how they live and to make any political choices concerning them. Making a profit is a disease in our society, based on specific organisations. A decent, ethical society would pay only marginal attention to profits. Take my university department [at the Massachusetts Institute of Technology]: a few scientists work very hard to earn lots of money, but they are considered a little odd and slightly deranged, almost pathological cases. Most of the academic community is more concerned about trying to break new ground, out of intellectual interest and for the general good.

In a recent tribute, [sociologist and UN representative] Jean Ziegler wrote: "There have been three forms of totalitarian rule: Stalinism, Nazism and now Tina [the acronym from British prime minister Margaret Thatcher's statement, 'There is no alternative'—that is, to economic liberalism and global free-market capitalism]." Do you think they can be compared?

I don't think they should be placed on the same footing. Fighting Tina means confronting a system of intellectual control that cannot be compared with concentration camps or the gulag. US policies provoke massive opposition all over the world. . . . Latin America, Argentina and Venezuela have thrown out the International Monetary Fund. Washington can no longer stage military takeovers in Latin America as it did 20 or 30 years ago. The whole continent now rejects the neo-liberal economic programme forcibly imposed on it by the US in the 1980s and 1990s. There are signs of the same opposition to the global market all over the world.

The Global Justice Movement, which attracts a great deal of media attention at each World Social Forum (WSF), is hard at work all year. It is a new departure and perhaps the start of a real International [effort]. But its main objective is to prove that there is an alternative. What better example of a different form of global exchange than the WSF itself. Hostile media organisations refer to anyone opposed to the neo-liberal global market as antis, whereas in fact they are campaigning for another form of global market, for the people.

We can easily observe the contrast between the two parties because their meetings coincide. We have the World Economic Forum, in Davos [Switzerland], which is striving to promote global economic integration but in the exclusive interests of financiers, banks and pension funds. These organisations happen to control the media too. They defend their conception of global integration, which is there to serve investors. The dominant media consider that this form of integration is the only one to qualify as globalisation. Davos is a good example of how ideological propaganda works in democratic societies. It is so effective that even WSF participants sometimes accept the ill-intentioned "anti" label. I spoke at the Forum in Porto Alegre [Brazil] and took part in the Via Campesina [global movement of small-scale farmers] conference. They represent the majority of the world's population.

Critics tend to lump you together with the anarchists and libertarian socialists. What would be the role of the state in a real democracy?

We are living here and now, not in some imaginary universe. And here and now there are tyrannical organisations—big corporations. They are the closest thing to a totalitarian institution. They are, to all intents and purposes, quite unaccountable to the general public or society as a whole. They behave like predators, preying on other smaller companies. People have only one means of defending themselves and that is the state. Nor is it a very effective shield because it is often closely linked to the predators. But there is a far from negligible difference. General Electric is accountable to no one, whereas the state must occasionally explain its actions to the public.

Once democracy has been enlarged far enough for citizens to control the means of production and trade, and they take part in the overall running and management of the environment in which they live, then the state will gradually be able to disappear. It will be replaced by voluntary associations at our place of work and where we live. . . .

Isn't it the case that all forms of autonomous organisation based on anarchist principles have ultimately collapsed?

There are no set anarchist principles, no libertarian creed to which we must all swear allegiance. Anarchism—at least as I understand it—is a movement that tries to identify organisations exerting authority and domination, to ask them to justify their actions and, if they are unable to do so, as often happens, to try to supersede them.

Far from collapsing, anarchism and libertarian thought are flourishing. They have given rise to real progress in many fields. Forms of oppression and injustice that were once barely recognised, less still disputed, are no longer allowed. That in itself is a success, a step forward for all humankind, certainly not a failure.

CHAPTER 3

Modern Democracy Beyond the West

Chapter Preface

Two-thirds of the world's 193 countries are democracies, and some 140 countries operate based on some form of democratic institutions. These democracies come in various forms from Sweden, which enjoys high voter participation and a vast complement of individual rights, to Iraq, an occupied and war-ravaged country that struggles to make its democratic institutions work. According to the *Economist*'s 2006 Democracy Index, more than half of the world's population lives in some type of democracy, but only 13 percent live in what are considered to be full democracies while the remaining 87 percent live in "flawed democracies" (38 percent), "hybrid regimes" (10 percent), or "authoritarian regimes" (38 percent).

What makes a country a "full democracy" or something else? The very use of such rankings has been met with criticism, particularly by those who fall low on the list. Some conservative Americans have dismissed this type of survey, arguing that it is not possible to rank Sweden, with its socialist democratic system of government and state regulation of media, as a democracy. But such a criticism confuses the ideas of republicanism with democracy, and perhaps conflates freedom and democracy. In fact, democracy around the world comes in various forms, and it is not only the type of democracy practiced by the United States, its critics say, that should be regarded as "true democracy."

The difficulty of deciding which countries are true democracies is compounded by the fact that there is no general consensus on what constitutes a democracy. According to professor William A. Cook, Israel, for example, which is commonly considered a democracy, should not be labeled a democracy at all because it does not fit the basic standards: It does not recognize the rights of Palestinians, its government does not have the consent of some over whom it wields power, it does not recognize the rights of all citizens that reside within the state, and it does not treat each of its citizens equally. Others, such as policy experts and authors Anatol Lieven and John Hulsman, have argued that American standards of democracy are too closely tied to American interests. For physicist and author Vandana Shiva, American-style democracy is to be rejected because it is market driven, making democracy synonymous with market capitalism and the interests of corporations over people.

In the twenty-first century if a country claims faithfulness to democratic principles, that country will tend to be considered politically legitimate to the rest of the world. Therefore many governments take pains to declare their democratic credentials. For example, some Muslim scholars have argued that Islam enshrines democratic values as a way of showing that Muslim countries are abiding by the principles of decency.

Detractors call much of this reaction a case of twisting the facts to appease Western power holders. The terrorist attacks on America on September 11, 2001, left the Muslim world feeling vulnerable to being criticized and thus there is a need to show that Muslim principles are just and legitimate. Some commentators suggest this may have been encouraged too by U.S. rhetoric suggesting that only if the nations of the world adopt the principles of democracy can they be considered peaceful. Political analyst Fareed Zakaria argues that the presidency of George W. Bush, with its focus on promoting democracy around the world, has done considerable damage by pushing this line of reasoning. In encouraging democracy rather than good governance, and by setting a poor example by restricting the freedoms of its own citizens, Zakaria says that the U.S. president has cheapened the idea of democracy rather than encouraged its adoption around the world.

The Universal Validity
of Democracy

Amartya Sen

Amartya Sen is a Nobel Prize-winning economist and professor at Cambridge University. In the following essay, Sen suggests that the rise of democracy may be seen as the most important development of the twentieth century. He examines democracy as a universal value by focusing on India's experience. He says first of all that democracy can be said to have universal value not because it is consented to universally but because people ev- erywhere have reason to see it as valuable. He goes on to show how democracy enriches the lives of its citizens, using India as a case study. He makes his now-famous statement that famines do not occur in democracies because democratic governments must win elections and face public criticism, and therefore have a strong incentive to avert famines and other catastrophes. Sen lists three ways in which democracy enhances the lives of the citizenry: democracy provides political freedom, which is part of human freedom in general; democracy encourages free expres- sion; and democracy provides citizens with the opportunity to learn from one another and to form social values and priorties.

In the summer of 1997, I was asked by a leading Japanese newspaper what I thought was the most important thing that had happened in the twentieth century. I found this to be an unusually thought-provoking question, since so many things of gravity have happened over the last hundred years. The European empires, especially the British and French ones that had so dominated the nineteenth century, came to an end. We witnessed two world wars. We saw the rise and fall of fascism and Nazism. The century witnessed the rise of com-

Amartya Sen, "Democracy as a Universal Value," *Journal of Democracy*, vol. 10, no. 3, 1999, pp. 3–17. Copyright © 1999 The Johns Hopkins University Press. Reproduced by permission.

munism, and its fall (as in the former Soviet bloc) or radical transformation (as in China). We also saw a shift from the economic dominance of the West to a new economic balance much more dominated by Japan and East and Southeast Asia. Even though that region is going through some financial and economic problems right now, this is not going to nullify the shift in the balance of the world economy that has occurred over many decades (in the case of Japan, through nearly the entire century). The past hundred years are not lacking in important events.

Nevertheless, among the great variety of developments that have occurred in the twentieth century, I did not, ultimately, have any difficulty in choosing one as the preeminent development of the period: the rise of democracy. This is not to deny that other occurrences have also been important, but I would argue that in the distant future, when people look back at what happened in this century, they will find it difficult not to accord primacy to the emergence of democracy as the preeminently acceptable form of governance.

The idea of democracy originated, of course, in ancient Greece, more than two millennia ago. Piecemeal efforts at democratization were attempted elsewhere as well, including in India. But it is really in ancient Greece that the idea of democracy took shape and was seriously put into practice (albeit on a limited scale), before it collapsed and was replaced by more authoritarian and asymmetric forms of government. There were no other kinds anywhere else.

The Development of Democracy

Thereafter, democracy as we know it took a long time to emerge. Its gradual—and ultimately triumphant—emergence as a working system of governance was bolstered by many developments, from the signing of the Magna Carta in 1215, to the French and the American Revolutions in the eighteenth century, to the widening of the franchise in Europe and North

America in the nineteenth century. It was in the twentieth century, however, that the idea of democracy became established as the "normal" form of government to which any nation is entitled—whether in Europe, America, Asia, or Africa.

The idea of democracy as a universal commitment is quite new, and it is quintessentially a product of the twentieth century. The rebels who forced restraint on the king of England through the Magna Carta saw the need as an entirely local one. In contrast, the American fighters for independence and the revolutionaries in France contributed greatly to an understanding of the need for democracy as a general system. Yet the focus of their practical demands remained quite local—confined, in effect, to the two sides of the North Atlantic, and founded on the special economic, social, and political history of the region.

Throughout the nineteenth century, theorists of democracy found it quite natural to discuss whether one country or another was "fit for democracy." This thinking changed only in the twentieth century, with the recognition that the question itself was wrong: A country does not have to be deemed fit *for* democracy; rather, it has to become fit *through* democracy. This is indeed a momentous change, extending the potential reach of democracy to cover billions of people, with their varying histories and cultures and disparate levels of affluence.

It was also in this century that people finally accepted that "franchise for all adults" must mean *all*—not just men but also women. When in January of this year [1999] I had the opportunity to meet Ruth Dreyfuss, the president of Switzerland and a woman of remarkable distinction, it gave me occasion to recollect that only a quarter century ago Swiss women could not even vote. We have at last reached the point of recognizing that the coverage of universality, like the quality of mercy, is not strained.

I do not deny that there are challenges to democracy's claim to universality. These challenges come in many shapes and forms—and from different directions. Indeed, that is part of the subject of this essay. I have to examine the claim of democracy as a universal value and the disputes that surround that claim. Before I begin that exercise, however, it is necessary to grasp clearly the sense in which democracy has become a dominant belief in the contemporary world.

In any age and social climate, there are some sweeping beliefs that seem to command respect as a kind of general rule—like a "default" setting in a computer program; they are considered right *unless* their claim is somehow precisely negated. While democracy is not yet universally practiced, nor indeed uniformly accepted, in the general climate of world opinion, democratic governance has now achieved the status of being taken to be generally right. The ball is very much in the court of those who want to rubbish democracy to provide justification for that rejection.

This is a historic change from not very long ago, when the advocates of democracy for Asia or Africa had to argue for democracy with their backs to the wall. While we still have reason enough to dispute those who, implicitly or explicitly, reject the need for democracy, we must also note clearly how the general climate of opinion has shifted from what it was in previous centuries. We do not have to establish afresh, each time, whether such and such a country (South Africa, or Cambodia, or Chile) is "fit for democracy" (a question that was prominent in the discourse of the nineteenth century); we now take that for granted. This recognition of democracy as a universally relevant system, which moves in the direction of its acceptance as a universal value, is a major revolution in thinking, and one of the main contributions of the twentieth century. It is in this context that we have to examine the question of democracy as a universal value.

The Indian Experience

How well has democracy worked? While no one really questions the role of democracy in, say, the United States or Britain or France, it is still a matter of dispute for many of the poorer countries in the world. This is not the occasion for a detailed examination of the historical record, but I would argue that democracy has worked well enough.

India, of course, was one of the major battlegrounds of this debate. In denying Indians independence, the British expressed anxiety over the Indians' ability to govern themselves. India was indeed in some disarray in 1947, the year it became independent. It had an untried government, an undigested partition, and unclear political alignments, combined with widespread communal violence and social disorder. It was hard to have faith in the future of a united and democratic India. And yet, half a century later, we find a democracy that has, taking the rough with the smooth, worked remarkably well. Political differences have been largely tackled within the constitutional guidelines, and governments have risen and fallen according to electoral and parliamentary rules. An ungainly, unlikely, inelegant combination of differences, India nonetheless survives and functions remarkably well as a political unit with a democratic system. Indeed, it is held together by its working democracy.

India has also survived the tremendous challenge of dealing with a variety of major languages and a spectrum of religions. Religious and communal differences are, of course, vulnerable to exploitation by sectarian politicians, and have indeed been so used on several occasions (including in recent months), causing massive consternation in the country. Yet the fact that consternation greets sectarian violence and that condemnation of such violence comes from all sections of the country ultimately provides the main democratic guarantee against the narrowly factional exploitation of sectarianism. This is, of course, essential for the survival and prosperity of a country as remarkably varied as India, which is home not only to a Hindu majority, but to the world's third largest Muslim population, to millions of Christians and Buddhists, and to most of the world's Sikhs, Parsees, and Jains.

Democracy and Economic Development

It is often claimed that nondemocratic systems are better at bringing about economic development. This belief sometimes goes by the name of "the Lee hypothesis," due to its advocacy by Lee Kuan Yew, the leader and former president of Singapore. He is certainly right that some disciplinarian states (such as South Korea, his own Singapore, and postreform China) have had faster rates of economic growth than many less authoritarian ones (including India, Jamaica, and Costa Rica). The "Lee hypothesis," however, is based on sporadic empiricism, drawing on very selective and limited information, rather than on any general statistical testing over the wide-ranging data that are available. A general relation of this kind cannot be established on the basis of very selective evidence. For example, we cannot really take the high economic growth of Singapore or China as "definitive proof" that authoritarianism does better in promoting economic growth, any more than we can draw the opposite conclusion from the fact that Botswana, the country with the best record of economic growth in Africa, indeed with one of the finest records of economic growth in the whole world, has been an oasis of democracy on that continent over the decades. We need more systematic empirical studies to sort out the claims and counterclaims.

There is, in fact, no convincing general evidence that authoritarian governance and the suppression of political and civil rights are really beneficial to economic development. Indeed, the general statistical picture does not permit any such induction. Systematic empirical studies (for example, by Robert Barro or by Adam Przeworski) give no real support to the claim that there is a general conflict between political rights and economic performance. The directional linkage seems to depend on many other circumstances, and while some statistical investigations note a weakly negative relation, others find a strongly positive one. If all the comparative studies are viewed together, the hypothesis that there is no clear relation between economic growth and democracy in *either* direction remains extremely plausible. Since democracy and political liberty have importance in themselves, the case for them therefore remains untarnished.

The question also involves a fundamental issue of methods of economic research. We must not only look at statistical connections, but also examine and scrutinize the *causal* processes that are involved in economic growth and development. The economic policies and circumstances that led to the economic success of countries in East Asia are by now reasonably well understood. While different empirical studies have varied in emphasis, there is by now broad consensus on a list of "helpful policies" that includes openness to competition, the use of international markets, public provision of incentives for investment and export, a high level of literacy and schooling, successful land reforms, and other social opportunities that widen participation in the process of economic expansion. There is no reason at all to assume that any of these policies is inconsistent with greater democracy and had to be forcibly sustained by the elements of authoritarianism that happened to be present in South Korea or Singapore or China. Indeed, there is overwhelming evidence to show that what is needed for generating faster economic growth is a friendlier economic climate rather than a harsher political system.

To complete this examination, we must go beyond the narrow confines of economic growth and scrutinize the broader demands of economic development, including the need for economic and social security. In that context, we have to look at the connection between political and civil rights, on the one hand, and the prevention of major economic disasters, on the other. Political and civil rights give people the opportunity to draw attention forcefully to general needs and to demand appropriate public action. The response of a government to the acute suffering of its people often depends on the pressure that is put on it. The exercise of political rights (such as voting, criticizing, protesting, and the like) can make a real difference to the political incentives that operate on a government.

I have discussed elsewhere the remarkable fact that, in the terrible history of famines in the world, no substantial famine has ever occurred in any independent and democratic country with a relatively free press. We cannot find exceptions to this rule, no matter where we look: the recent famines of Ethiopia, Somalia, or other dictatorial regimes; famines in the Soviet Union in the 1930s; China's 1958–61 famine with the failure of the Great Leap Forward; or earlier still, the famines in Ireland or India under alien rule. China, although it was in many ways doing much better economically than India, still managed (unlike India) to have a famine, indeed the largest recorded famine in world history: Nearly 30 million people died in the famine of 1958–61, while faulty governmental policies remained uncorrected for three full years. The policies went uncriticized because there were no opposition parties in parliament, no free press, and no multiparty elections. Indeed, it is precisely this lack of challenge that allowed the deeply defective policies to continue even though they were killing millions each year. The same can be said about the world's two contemporary famines, occurring right now in North Korea and Sudan.

Famines are often associated with what look like natural disasters, and commentators often settle for the simplicity of explaining famines by pointing to these events: the floods in China during the failed Great Leap Forward, the droughts in Ethiopia, or crop failures in North Korea. Nevertheless, many countries with similar natural problems, or even worse ones, manage perfectly well, because a responsive government intervenes to help alleviate hunger. Since the primary victims of a famine are the indigent, deaths can be prevented by re-creating incomes (for example, through employment programs), which makes food accessible to potential famine victims. Even the poorest democratic countries that have faced terrible droughts or floods or other natural disasters (such as India in 1973, or Zimbabwe and Botswana in the early 1980s) have been able to feed their people without experiencing a famine.

Famines are easy to prevent if there is a serious effort to do so, and a democratic government, facing elections and criticisms from opposition parties and independent newspapers, cannot help but make such an effort. Not surprisingly, while India continued to have famines under British rule right up to independence (the last famine, which I witnessed as a child, was in 1943, four years before independence), they disappeared suddenly with the establishment of a multiparty democracy and a free press. . . .

Indeed, the issue of famine is only one example of the reach of democracy, though it is, in many ways, the easiest case to analyze. The positive role of political and civil rights applies to the prevention of economic and social disasters in general. When things go fine and everything is routinely good, this instrumental role of democracy may not be particularly missed. It is when things get fouled up, for one reason or another, that the political incentives provided by democratic governance acquire great practical value.

There is, I believe, an important lesson here. Many economic technocrats recommend the use of economic incentives (which the market system provides) while ignoring political incentives (which democratic systems could guarantee). This is to opt for a deeply unbalanced set of ground rules. The protective power of democracy may not be missed much when a country is lucky enough to be facing no serious calamity, when everything is going quite smoothly. Yet the danger of insecurity, arising from changed economic or other circumstances, or from uncorrected mistakes of policy, can lurk behind what looks like a healthy state.

The recent problems of East and Southeast Asia bring out, among other things, the penalties of undemocratic governance. This is so in two striking respects. First, the development of the financial crisis in some of these economies (including South Korea, Thailand, Indonesia) has been closely linked to the lack of transparency in business, in particular the lack of public participation in reviewing financial arrangements. The absence of an effective democratic forum has been central to this failing. Second, once the financial crisis led to a general economic recession, the protective power of democracy—not unlike that which prevents famines in democratic countries—was badly missed in a country like Indonesia. The newly dispossessed did not have the hearing they needed. . . .

A fall in total gross national product of, say, 10 percent may not look like much if it follows in the wake of a growth rate of 5 or 10 percent every year over the past few decades, and yet that decline can decimate lives and create misery for millions if the burden of contraction is not widely shared but allowed to be heaped on those—the unemployed or the economically redundant—who can least bear it. The vulnerable in Indonesia may not have missed democracy when things went up and up, but that lacuna kept their voice low and muffled as the unequally shared crisis developed. The protective role of democracy is strongly missed when it is most needed. . . .

The Functions of Democracy

What exactly is democracy? We must not identify democracy with majority rule. Democracy has complex demands, which certainly include voting and respect for election results, but it also requires the protection of liberties and freedoms, respect for legal entitlements, and the guaranteeing of free discussion and uncensored distribution of news and fair comment. Even elections can be deeply defective if they occur without the different sides getting an adequate opportunity to present their respective cases, or without the electorate enjoying the freedom to obtain news and to consider the views of the competing protagonists. Democracy is a demanding system, and not just a mechanical condition (like majority rule) taken in isolation.

Viewed in this light, the merits of democracy and its claim as a universal value can be related to certain distinct virtues that go with its unfettered practice. Indeed, we can distinguish three different ways in which democracy enriches the lives of the citizens. First, political freedom is a part of human freedom in general, and exercising civil and political rights is a crucial part of good lives of individuals as social beings. Political and social participation has *intrinsic value* for human life and well-being. To be prevented from participation in the political life of the community is a major deprivation.

Second, as I have just discussed (in disputing the claim that democracy is in tension with economic development), democracy has an important *instrumental value* in enhancing the hearing that people get in expressing and supporting their claims to political attention (including claims of economic needs). Third—and this is a point to be explored further—the practice of democracy gives citizens an opportunity to learn from one another, and helps society to form its values and priorities. Even the idea of "needs," including the understanding of "economic needs," requires public discussion and exchange of information, views, and analyses. In this sense, democracy has *constructive* importance, in addition to its intrinsic value for the lives of the citizens and its instrumental importance in political decisions. The claims of democracy as a universal value have to take note of this diversity of considerations.

Liberal Democracy Is Culturally Particular

Bhikhu Parekh

Bhikhu Parekh is a political theorist who holds the Centennial Professorship at the Centre for the Study of Global Governance at the London School of Economics. In his article, Parekh argues that liberal democracy is liberalized democracy, that is, democracy defined and structured within the limits set by liberalism. He outlines the constitutive features of liberalism and shows how they determined the form and content of democracy and gave rise to liberal democracy as it is known today. He then goes on to argue that liberal democracy is specific to a particular cultural context and cannot claim universal validity. This, however, does not lead to cultural relativism, he says, as it is possible to formulate universal principles that every good government should respect.

Having briefly highlighted the basic features of liberal democracy, we may ask if the liberal democrat is right to claim universal validity for it and to maintain that all political systems failing to measure up to it are to that extent improperly constituted and defective.

Liberal democracy defines democracy within the limits of liberalism and represents one way of combining the two. There is no obvious reason why a political system may not combine them differently. It might assign them *equal* importance and use each to limit the excesses of the other. While continuing to insulate the government against popular pressure, it might provide ways of making it more responsive. Without damaging the government's right to govern, it might provide a greater network of channels for popular participation. And while recognizing the importance of protecting basic human rights, it might define and limit them in the light of a constantly evolving democratic consensus.

Or a political system might be democratically liberal rather than a liberal democracy, making democracy the dominant partner and defining liberalism within the limits set by it. Like liberal democracy such a political system cherishes and respects individuals, but defines them and their rights in social terms. It establishes a healthier balance between the individual and the community, aims at a fairer distribution of the opportunities required for full citizenship, extends participation to major areas of economic and political life, and opens up new centres of power. The early socialists, the young [Karl] Marx, C. B. Macpherson and many European socialist parties today advocate such a democratically constituted liberal polity in preference to liberal democracy. Democratic liberalism is fairly close to social democracy and represents a partial transcendence of liberalism.

How a polity [a political group or organization] combines liberalism and democracy or how liberal and democratic it chooses to be depends on its history, traditions, values, problems and needs. A polity is not a chance and fluctuating collection of individuals but has a history and a character, and needs to work out its political destiny in its own distinct way. As we saw, the Athenian democracy could not be revived in the modern age, and modern western societies had to evolve their own distinct forms of democracy. What is true of the west is equally true of the rest of the world. To insist on the universality of liberal democracy is to deny the west's own historical experiences and to betray the liberal principles of mutual respect and love of cultural diversity. It imposes on other countries systems of government unsuited to their talents and skills, destroys the coherence and integrity of their ways of life, and reduces them to mimics, unable and unwill-

125

ing to be true either to their traditions or to the imported norms. The cultural havoc caused by colonialism should alert us to the dangers of an overzealous imposition of liberal democracy.

Liberal democracy is a product of, and designed to cope with, the political problems thrown up by the post-seventeenth-century individualist society. As such there are at least two types of polity where its relevance would seem to be considerably limited, namely cohesive polities with a strong sense of community and multi-communal polities. Let us take each in turn.

Cohesive Communal Societies

There are polities in the world which have a strong sense of community based on a widely shared and deeply held conception of the good life. Saudi Arabia, Kuwait and several Middle Eastern and African polities belong to this category. They define the individual in communal terms and do not regard the atomic liberal individual as the basic unit of society. A poignant recent example illustrates the point well. A middle-aged Bangladeshi entitled to settle in Britain had two sons whom he was at liberty to bring into the country. When the immigration officer asked him if they were his sons, he replied in the affirmative. It later transpired that they were his dead brother's sons. Since they were not *his* children, the officer accused him of making a fraudulent claim. The Bangladeshi argued that his dead brother was not 'really' separate from him, that their children had all grown up together as brothers and sisters entitled to the equal attention and affection of all adults, that each adult in the family had a moral obligation to look after the children of all of them, that this was how his society was constituted, and that he had additionally given a pledge to his dying brother to treat his children as his own. Since he saw no difference whatsoever between his own and his brother's sons, he chose to bring in the latter. When the bemused officer proved unrelenting and insisted that the Bangladeshi could only bring in his own two sons, the latter offered to bring in one of his own and one of his dead brother's sons. Since the quota of two children was not exceeded, he could not understand why it mattered to the British government how it was made up. He also argued that his 'selfishness' would not be forgiven by his community and his dead brother's family, and nor would he be able to live with himself, if he did not bring in at least one of his dead brother's sons. In this conflict between the two different conceptions of the self, neither side could make sense of the other. Being used to the liberal view which he regarded as self-evident, and convinced that it was his duty to enforce the law, the immigration officer deported the Bangladeshi back to his country with the instruction that he was never to be allowed into Britain.

The point of this example is that different societies define and individuate people differently. They also therefore define freedom, equality, rights, property, justice, loyalty, power and authority differently. For example, in a traditional Muslim society every man is required to consider a portion of his property as belonging to others. He has a duty to use it for their benefit and is not allowed to deny food or shelter to a hungry man or to a stranger. The latter does not have a *right* to food or shelter, but the host has a most stringent *duty* to provide these. No one talks of rights, yet almost everyone's needs are met. No one uses the language of 'justice', the term for which some of these societies have no equivalent words, but most of their members receive their due and the distribution of goods is generally equitable. In short, the liberal principle of individuation and other liberal ideas are culturally and historically specific. As such a political system based on them cannot claim universal validity.

The non-liberal but not necessarily illiberal societies we are discussing cherish and wish to preserve their ways of life.

Like most pre-modern societies they are communally oriented and believe that their members' 'rights' may be legitimately restricted in the larger interest of the traditional way of life. Most of them allow freedom of speech and expression, but not the freedom to mock and ridicule their sacred texts, practices, beliefs and rituals. They restrict the right to property and to trade and commerce lest it should undermine the ethos of social solidarity and the ethic of communal obligation lying at the basis of their ways of life. They restrict travel, immigration and the freedom to buy and sell land for basically the same reasons. Liberals find such restrictions unacceptable, but most members of traditional societies do not. Unless we assume that liberalism represents the final truth about human beings, we cannot indiscriminately condemn societies that do not conform to it. This is particularly so today when the liberal societies are themselves beginning to wonder if they have not carried individualism too far, and how they can create genuine communities without which individuals lack roots and stability. Community implies shared values and a common way of life, and is incompatible with the more or less unrestrained rights of its members to do as they please. It is striking that many a communitarian theorist has suggested restrictions on pornography, freedom of expression and immigration that are not very different from those characteristic of traditional societies.

It is, of course, true that some traditional societies have grossly outrageous practices and customs which obviously need to be changed, preferably by internal and, when necessary, by a judiciously applied external pressure. The question we are considering, however, is not how to improve their ways of life but whether they must adopt, and be condemned for refusing to adopt, liberal democratic institutions. It is difficult to see how this question can be answered in the affirmative. As long as their forms of government are acceptable to their people and meet the basic conditions of good government, to which I shall return later, they must be at liberty to work out their political destiny themselves.

Multi-Communal Societies

We have so far talked about cohesive communities. We may now briefly consider multi-communal societies; that is, societies which comprise several cohesive and self-conscious communities each seeking to preserve its traditional way of life. Several third world countries belong to this category. Neither the Athenian model, which presupposes a community, nor the liberal model, which presupposes none, applies to such multi-communal societies, with the result that the theoretical problems raised by their experiences have received little attention in much of western democratic theory.

The point will become clear if we look at the case of India, one of the most ethnically and religiously diverse societies in the world. The colonial state in India left the long-established communities more or less alone, accepted their 'laws' and practices, and superimposed on them a minimal body of mainly criminal laws. Unlike its European counterpart, it permitted a plurality of legal systems and shared its 'sovereignty' with the autonomous and largely self-governing communities.

Post-independence India only partially rationalized the colonial state and remains a highly complex polity. It has a uniform body of criminal but not civil laws. Muslims continue to be governed by their own personal laws, which the state enforces but with which it does not interfere. The tribals too are governed by their separate laws, and the state has committed itself to making no changes in the practices and laws of the Christians without their explicit consent and approval. The Parsis are subject to the same civil laws as the rest of non-Muslim Indians, but the interpretation and application of the laws is in some cases left to their *panchayats* or community councils. Thus the ordinary civil courts will hear a Parsi divorce case, but leave it to the Parsi *panchayat* to decide on the machinery of reconciliation and the amount of alimony. The Indian state is thus both an association of individuals and a community of communities, recognizing both individuals and communities as bearers of rights. The criminal law recognizes only individuals, whereas the civil law recognizes most minority communities as distinct legal subjects. This makes India a liberal democracy of a very peculiar kind.

It is tempting to say, as many Indian and foreign commentators have said, that the Indian state is too 'deeply embedded' in society and too 'plural' and 'chaotic' to be considered a properly constituted state or a state in the 'true' sense of the word. But such a view is obviously too superficial and ethnocentric to be satisfactory. There is no reason why we should accept the view that the modern western constitution of the state is the only true or proper one, and deny India and other non-western societies the right to indigenize the imported institution of the state and even to evolve their own alternative political formations. Rather than insist that the state *must* be autonomous and separate from society, and then set about finding ways of restoring it to the people, we might argue that it should not be separated from society in the first instance. And rather than insist that the state *must* have a uniform legal system, we might argue that it should be free to allow its constituent communities to retain their different laws and practices, so long as these conform to clearly laid down and nationally accepted principles of justice and fairness. Thus the law might require that a divorced wife must be provided for, but leave the different communities free to decide whether the husband, his family, or his community as a whole should arrange for her maintenance, so long as the arrangements are foolproof and not open to abuse and arbitrary alternation. If the multi-communal polities are to hold together and to avoid the all too familiar eruptions of inter- and intra-communal violence, they need to be extremely sensitive to the traditions, values and levels of development of their constituent communities, and may find the institutions and practices developed in socially homogeneous liberal societies deeply subversive.

Like the concepts of the individual, right, property and so on, such institutions as elections, multiple political parties, the separation of powers and the abstract state too cannot be universalized. Elections of the western type impose a crushing financial burden on poor countries and encourage the all too familiar forms of corruption. In an ethnically and religiously diverse society lacking shared values, or in a society unused to discussing its differences in public and articulating them in neat ideological terms, elections might also prove deeply divisive, generate artificial ideological rigidities, release powerful aggressive impulses and channel them into dangerous and unaccustomed directions. Such societies might be better off sticking to or evolving consensual and less polarized ways of selecting their government and conducting their affairs. What is true of elections is equally true of other liberal democratic institutions and practices.

This is not to say that liberal democratic institutions have no value for non-western societies, rather that the latter have to determine the value themselves in the light of their cultural resources, needs and circumstances, and that they cannot mechanically transplant them. As a matter of fact, many third world countries have tried all manner of political experiments, some successful and others disastrous. Thanks to the profoundly mistaken belief, partly self-induced and partly encouraged by western governments and developmental experts, that their experiments were 'deviations' from the 'true' liberal democratic model and symptomatic of their immaturity and backwardness, they often undertook them without much zeal and self-confidence and abandoned them prematurely. Their political predicament is very like their linguistic predicament. They abandoned their traditional languages, which they well knew how to speak, in favour of the 'proper' and 'respectable' languages of their colonial rulers, which they would never adequately master.

Liberalism at Odds with Cultural Values

It would appear that the democratic part of liberal democracy, consisting in such things as free elections, free speech and the right to equality, has proved far more attractive outside the west and is more universalizable than the liberal component. Millions in non-western societies demand democracy, albeit in suitably indigenized forms, whereas they tend to shy away from liberalism as if they instinctively felt it to be subversive of what they most valued and cherished. This is not because it leads to capitalism, for many of them welcome the latter, but because the third world countries feel that the liberal view of the world and way of life is at odds with their deepest aspirations and self-conceptions. As they understand it, liberalism breaks up the community, undermines the shared body of ideas and values, places the isolated individual above the community, encourages the ethos and ethic of aggressive self-assertion, rejects traditional wisdom and common sense in the name of scientific reason, and weakens the spirit of mutual accommodation and adjustment. Non-western societies wonder why they cannot import such western technology and expertise as they need while rejecting some of its liberal values and suitably indigenizing some of its democratic practices. They might be proved wrong and may suffer as a result. But forcing them into the standard liberal democratic mould is not without its heavy human cost either.

To reject the universalist claims of liberal democracy is not to endorse the crude relativist view that a country's political system is its own business and above criticism, and that western experiences have no relevance outside the west. In an increasingly interdependent world every country's internal affairs impinge on others and are a matter of general concern.

The dissidents, the oppressed minorities and the ill-treated masses the world over appeal to international public opinion for support, and we cannot respond to them without the help of general principles to guide our judgements and actions. Thanks to the widening of our moral consciousness, we feel morally concerned about human suffering even when our help is not directly asked for. And thanks to the increasing de-mystification of the modern state, we are beginning to realize that its citizens are not its property, that it is accountable to humankind for the way it treats them, and that it must be opened up to external scrutiny. All this calls for a body of moral and political principles that are both universally valid and capable of accommodating cultural diversity and autonomy. We need to work out the minimum conditions or principles of good government and leave different countries free to evolve their own appropriate forms of government compatible with these regulative principles.

Democracy as Universal Principle or Ethno-Centric Bias?

Since we cannot here pursue this large and complex question, a few general remarks will have to suffice. Universally valid regulative principles cannot be laid down by western governments, let alone by a philosopher, both because they are bound to be infected by an ethnocentric bias and because they can have no authority over the rest of humankind. It is easy to be prescriptive, but such prescription have no meaning and force unless they resonate in the lives of, and evoke sympathetic responses in the minds of, those affected by them. The principles of good government can be genuinely universal (in their scope and content) *and* binding only if they are freely negotiated by all involved and grounded in a broad global consensus. It would be wholly naive to imagine that all governments and all men and women everywhere will ever agree on them. What we can legitimately hope and strive for is a broad cross-cultural consensus commanding varying degrees of universal support. As individuals and groups in different parts of the world invoke it in their internal struggles, and as the rest of the world responds to them, the consensus acquires depth and vitality, becomes an acceptable political currency, strikes roots in popular consciousness, and acquires new adherents. This is broadly how almost all our moral principles have evolved and acquired authority. And this is also how the 1948 United Nations [UN] Declaration of Human Rights has acquired its current appeal. A pious statement of good intentions when first formulated in the aftermath of the second world war, it was increasingly invoked by the leaders of colonial struggles for independence and oppressed minorities, and over time became an important part of domestic and international morality.

The UN Declaration is a complex document and articulated at three different levels. First, it lays down the general principles every government should satisfy. Secondly, it translates these principles into the language of rights and lists different kinds of rights. Thirdly, it lays down institutions and practices that alone in its view can guarantee and protect these rights. The last two parts of it have a liberal democratic bias, the second part because of its use of the language of rights and the kinds of rights it stresses, and the third because the recommended institutions and practices presuppose and are specific to liberal democracy.

As for the general principles of the UN Declaration, they fall into two categories. Some are distinctly liberal and culturally specific; for example, the more or less unlimited right to freedom of expression and to private property, and the insistence that marriages must be based on the 'free and full consent' of the intending spouses. Other principles relate to vital human interests valued in almost all societies and have a genuinely universal core, such as respect for human life and dignity, equality before the law, equal protection of the law, fair trial and the protection of minorities. Liberalism does, of course, deeply cherish and place great value on these principles, but they are not unique to it. They were found in classical Athens and Rome and many a medieval kingdom, are emphasized in the sacred texts of all great religions, and were widely practised in many non-western societies. Indeed the record of some non-western societies in such areas as respect for human life and the protection of minorities, including Jews, is not only as good as but even better than that of the liberal west.

Evidence that the second category of principles laid down by the UN Declaration commands considerable universal support is threefold. First, the UN Declaration was signed by a large number of governments representing different cultures, geographical areas and political systems. Secondly, when the newly liberated Asian and African countries joined the UN they demanded amendments to its Declaration, which were accepted after much debate and embodied in the two International Covenants of 1966. The latter documents rejected the right to property and to full compensation in the event of nationalization, toned down the individualistic basis of the 1948 Declaration, and endorsed the occasional need to suspend individual rights in the national interest. However they not only left untouched but even strengthened what I have called the genuinely universal principles of the 1948 Declaration. Thirdly, people the world over have frequently appealed to these principles in their struggles against repressive governments. For their part the latter have almost invariably preferred to deny the existence of unacceptable practices rather than shelter behind relativism and cultural autonomy. In their own different ways both parties are thus beginning to accept the principles as the basis of good government, conferring on them the moral authority they otherwise cannot have. In other words, the principles are increasingly becoming 'a common standard of achievement for all peoples and nations' as the UN Declaration itself had hoped. As such they provide a most valuable basis for a freely negotiated and constantly evolving consensus on universally valid principles of good government.

Within the limits set by these principles, different countries should remain free to determine their own appropriate forms of government. They may choose liberal democracy, but if they do not their choice deserves respect and even encouragement. After all, liberals have always held, and rightly, that diversity is the precondition of progress and choice, and that truth can only emerge from a peaceful competition between different ways of life.

Israel Is Not a
Legitimate Democracy

William A. Cook

*William A. Cook is a professor of English at the University of La
Verne in California. In the following article, he questions the
conventional wisdom among American policy makers that Israel
is a bastion of democracy in the Middle East. A democracy, he
points out, must meet distinct criteria: It must recognize the
rights of humans relative to the government that acts in their
name; its government must serve through the consent of the governed; it must accept the rights of all resident citizens; and each
citizen must be treated equally under the law. And, in order to
put any of these rights into practice, it must have a legitimately
defined geographical boundary. Israel, Cook says, fails to meet
these criteria of a democracy because of its disputed boundaries,
its lack of constitution, and its treatment of those who dissent.
Upon scrutiny, Cook claims, Israel's government and institutions
simply do not express the ideals expressed in the U.S. Constitution, as many American supporters of the nation have been led
to believe.*

Israel's bulldozing of 62 shops in the village of Nazkt Issa,
north of Tulkarem next to the West Bank line with Israel on
Tuesday [January 21, 2003] and its refusal to allow International and Israeli peace activists to witness the devastation illustrates the total control of the military in what is supposed
to be a democratic state. Americans saw and heard little of
this action except that it was caused by the illegal establishment of the shops by Palestinians. In a democratic state, the
alleged "illegality" would be dealt with in a court of law, not
by an army protecting bulldozers from citizens throwing

William A. Cook, "Israeli Democracy: Fact or Fiction?" *CounterPunch*, January 25,
2003. www.counterpunch.org. Reproduced by permission.

stones. But Americans hear only what [Prime Minister Ariel] Sharon allows the corporate media in America to receive from his minions as he prevents outsiders from witnessing the demolition.

The impending Israeli elections and the plethora of commentary that touts Israel as the only bastion of Democracy in the mid-east warrants consideration of the truth of the claim in light of Tuesday's devastation. It would appear that the American public accepts the reality of Israel as a democratic state and finds comfort in its compatibility with American values. That comfort translates into approximately three billion dollars per year for Israel, more aid than any other country receives.

Criteria for Democracy

A true Democracy must meet two criteria: one philosophical that presents the logic of its argument in a declaration and/or constitution; the other practical that demonstrates how the Democracy implements legislation, distributes resources, and makes equitable all policies and procedures for all its citizens.

Democracy is first and foremost a concept, a philosophical understanding concerning the rights of humans relative to the government that acts in their name. A Democratic government serves through the manifest consent of the governed. That government receives its authority through the citizens in whom the right resides. Inherent in this philosophical understanding is the acceptance of the rights of all citizens that reside in a state: each and every citizen possesses the right to consent to the legitimacy of those who govern, and each and every citizen must receive equal treatment before the law.

For a state to claim a Democratic form of government, it must have an established geographic area accepted by other nations as legitimate and defined. The need for established borders is both obvious and necessary with necessity arising out of the obvious. Without borders, there can be no absolute determination of citizenry, and, therefore, no way to fulfill the establishment of the rights noted above. What has this to do with the Democratic state of Israel? Everything.

Israel Does Not Meet These Criteria

Israel has no accepted legitimate borders other than those provided to it by Resolution 181, according to Anthony D'Amato, Leighton Professor of Law at Northwestern University, in his brief "The Legal Boundaries of Israel in International Law": "The legal boundaries of Israel and Palestine were delimited in Resolution 181." Since the 1967 war, the borders of the current area controlled by Israel exceed those outlined by the UN [United Nations] in Resolution 181 of 1948 as the current incident in Nazkt Issa illustrates. Despite numerous resolutions from the UN demanding that Israel return to its proper borders, most especially Resolution 242, Israel defies the world body continuing to retain land illegally held. The reality of this dilemma is most manifest in the settlements. Here, Jews residing in Palestinian areas continue to vote while Palestinians literally surround them and cannot vote. Where is the state of Israel? A look at a map would make it appear that Israel has the spotted coloration of a Dalmatian. Clearly, those living under Israeli domination are not considered citizens of the state of Israel even though they reside within parameters controlled by Israel. Since they are not citizens of Israel, and since there is no Palestinian state, these people are without a country and, therefore, without rights; an untenable position for any group which is recognized as a distinct governing group by the UN through its election of the Palestinian Authority as its governing body. That election followed democratic procedures including the creation of a constitution and the international monitoring of the election process.

A Democratic state must declare the premises of its existence in a document or documents that present to the world the logic of its right to govern. That usually comes in the form of a constitution. Unlike the Palestinians, Israel has no constitution. Chuck Chriss, President of JIA [Jewish Internet Association] writes, "Israel has no written constitution, unlike the United States and most other democracies. There was supposed to be one. The Proclamation of Independence of the State of Israel calls for the preparation of a constitution, but it was never done." It's been more than 50 years since that "call." Why has Israel demurred on the creation of a constitution? Both Chriss in his article and Daniel J. Elazar, writing in "The Constitution of the State of Israel," point to the same dilemma: how to reconcile the secular and religious forces in Israel. Elazar states: "Israel has been unable to adopt a constitution full blown, not because it does not share the new society understanding of constitution as fundamental law, but because of a conflict over what constitutes fundamental law within Israeli society. Many religious Jews hold that the only real constitution for a Jewish state is the Torah and the Jewish law that flows from it. They not only see no need for a modern secular constitution, but even see in such a document a threat to the supremacy of the Torah."

The consequences of this divide can be seen in the discrepancies that exist in practice in Israel. While "the State of Israel is described in the Proclamation of Independence as both a Jewish State and a democracy with equal rights for all its citizens," the Foundation Law of 1980 makes clear that Israeli courts "shall decide [a case] in the light of the principles of freedom, justice, equity and peace of Israel's heritage." Without a written constitution, Israel relies on a set of laws encased in Israel's heritage, "some blatantly racist in their assignment of privilege based on religion," according to Tarif Abboushi writing in *CounterPunch* in June of 2002. But the structure of Israel's governing process that depends on a Knesset is also flawed. According to Chriss, "Members of the Knesset [MKs] are elected from lists proposed by the parties on a national basis. Following the election, the parties get to assign seats in the Knesset based on their proportion of the national vote, drawing from the party list. Thus, individual *MKs owe allegiance to the party chiefs and not directly to the electorate."* (Emphasis mine). He goes on to say, "This political system has resulted in some distortions in which Israeli law and government do not reflect the actual wishes of the voting population."

Different Standards for Arabs and Jews

For a state to claim a Democratic form of government, it must accept the equality of all residents within its borders as legitimate citizens regardless of race, ethnicity, creed, religion, political belief, or gender. For a state to claim it is Democratic and reserve the rights of citizenship to a select group negates its claim. It is an oxymoron to limit citizenship rights to Jews alone and call the state Democratic. As Joel Kovel has stated in *Tikkun,* "a democracy that is only to be for a certain people cannot exist, for the elementary reason that the modern democratic state is defined by its claims of universality." Yet this inherent contradiction exists in Israel. And this brings us from the philosophical phase to the practical one.

Daniel Elazar, reflecting on this conundrum in the post-modern era, notes that this "makes it impossible for the State to distinguish between the entitlements of Jewish citizens and others based upon obligations and performance; i.e., more benefits if one does military service than if one does not."

How does Israel implement the Democracy it claims to possess? First, any Jew from anywhere in the world can come to Israel and receive citizenship by virtue of his/her Jewishness. By contrast, a Muslim or Christian Palestinian living in exile because of the 1948 war cannot claim citizenship even though they were indigenous to the area, nor can their descendents claim citizenship. Second, ninety percent of the land in Israel is held in restrictive covenants, land initially owned by Palestinians for the most part, covenants that bar non-Jews from ownership including the Palestinians who hold a limited version of Israeli citizenship. Third, Israeli citizens who are Muslim or Christian do not share the rights accorded Jews who serve in the military, nor do they receive the benefits extended to those who serve in the military. Non-Jews are taxed differently than Israeli citizens and the neighborhoods in which they live receive less support. As recently as June 12, 2002, Paul Martin writing for the *Washington Times* noted "Israeli Arabs are trying to strike down a new law reducing family benefits, arguing that it has deliberately been drafted in a way that will affect Arabs more harshly than Jews."

While Arabs constitute 20% of the population within Israel, their voice in government is limited. Recently, an "expert" working for the General Security Service submitted his "expert opinion" to the Central Election Committee that undertook to disqualify Azmi Bishara and other Arab MKs from taking part in the election. This action would have deprived the Arabs of a voice in the Knesset if it had not been overturned by the Israeli court. The reality of Israeli political parties virtually assures non-representation of the Palestinians in the governing process. Even with Bishara permitted to run, the voice of the Palestinians is muted. As Uri Avnery noted recently, "One glance at the political map shows that without the Arab votes, no left-wing coalition has any chance of forming a government not today, nor in the forseeable future. This means that without the Arabs, the Left cannot even dictate terms for its participation in a coalition dominated by the Right."

Human Rights Abuses

Perhaps the most graphic illustration of the non-democracy that exists in Israel comes from Human Rights Watch [HRW] and the US State Department reports published in Jurist Law. The range of abuses listed by the State Department includes detainees beaten by police, poor prison conditions that did not meet international standards, detainees held without charge, holding of detainees as bargaining chips, refusal to allow access to [imprisoned sheikh Abdel Karim] Obeid by the Red Cross, imposition of heavier sentences on Arabs than Jews, interference with private rights, etc., and finally, "Trafficking in women for the purpose of forced prostitution is a continuing problem."

Human Rights Watch offers a litany of abuses, many more serious than those proferred by the Department of State: Israel has maintained the "liquidation" policy targeting individuals without trial by jury, lack of investigations to determine responsibility for killings and shootings, increased use of heavy weaponry, including F-16 fighter jets, etc., against "Palestinian police stations, security offices, prisons, and other installations." HRW also references the Israeli Information Center for Human Rights in the occupied Territories for the wanton killing of civilians by settlers. The listing is too extensive to offer in its totality here.

As I mentioned at the outset of this article, the American public hears constant reference to Israel as the only democratic nation in the mid-east. They receive little or no information about the accuracy of that statement. Yet Americans accept this administration's and past administrations' support of Israel in large measure because they believe that it reflects the ideals expressed in the American Constitution and they are willing to spend their tax dollars in support of those ideals. In reality, American democracy and Israeli democracy are decidedly distinct.

Democracy cannot exist in ignorance of policies, processes, and actions undertaken on behalf of the people including the refusal to admit citizens to areas like Nazkt Issa where non-democratic action exists. Silence by the peoples' representatives concerning reasons for actions taken in their name corrodes democracy. Americans have not been told, for example, that American authorities removed 8000 pages of information from the 12,000 provided by the Iraqi government to the UN

Inspectors, according to former MP Anthony Wedgewood Benn in an interview on BBC January 12th, pages removed to protect corporations that provided Iraq with chemicals and other material that could be used to develop WMD [weapons of mass destruction]. *Die Tageszeitung*, a Berlin Daily, reported the names of the corporations that acted with the government's approval through the '80s and up to 1991 supplying Saddam with nuclear, chemical, biological and missile technology. An extensive report on the chemicals sent to Iraq by the US was disclosed in the *Sunday Herald* by Neil Mackay and Felicity Arbuthnot, but received little press beyond this paper. How can the American people respond intelligently to the designs of this administration against Iraq without knowing how Iraq obtained its capability to develop WMD and the reasons for developing them?

Similarly, Israel cannot restrict its citizens, including peace activists, or its American supporters, from knowing how it acts relative to Palestinians by preventing reporters or activists from describing what is done in their name. Preventing the UN investigation of the Jenin "massacre" is only one example. Restricting journalists from occupied territory is another. Preventing Israeli and international peace activists from Nazkt Issa is the most recent.

While the founding fathers' verbalized the concepts and ideals that are the foundation of American Democracy in the Declaration of Independence and the Constitution, the full implementation of those ideals took many, many years to bring to fruition: a Civil War that freed slaves more than 70 years after the creation of the nation, Women's Rights more than 120 years after the founding, and the Civil Rights Acts of the '50s and '60s more than 150 years after its birth. That, however, is not a reason for Israel, or any nation moving toward a democratic status, to delay implementation of equal rights for all of their citizens; rather it is a demonstration of the necessity to introduce and ensure equity from the outset.

The World Does Not Need American-Style Democracy

Anatol Lieven and John Hulsman

Anatol Lieven is a senior research fellow at the New America Foundation in Washington, D.C., author of America Right or Wrong: An Anatomy of American Nationalism, *and a former journalist specializing in foreign affairs. John Hulsman is a contributing editor at the* National Interest. *In the following essay, the authors argue that it is a mistake for the United States to think that spreading democracy around the world is a noble and worthwhile goal. The assumption, they say, is that adopting American-style democracy would put countries on a path to prosperity and stability. But the authors assert that what it forgets is that there are cultural and economic factors that make democracy not nearly as attractive to the rest of the world as most Americans would assume, and many people, such as those in the Middle East, might not think that democracy is in their best interest. Rather than demonize a country for rejecting democracy, the United States should consider whether the country is in fact expressing the will of its people.*

A certain awareness of the limits on American power is growing among the wiser U.S. policy elites as a result of the disasters into which the [George W.] Bush administration has led the United States. Even in these circles, however, a very widespread belief exists that in the former Soviet Union and in the Muslim world, America can compensate for these weaknesses by encouraging the spread of democracy. The idea that "democracy" will solve all problems is also used as a conscious or unconscious excuse to avoid having to think seriously about negotiating compromise solutions to a range of disputes in

Anatol Lieven, "The Folly of Exporting Democracy," *TomPaine.com*, September 12, 2006. Reproduced by permission.

the Middle East, and especially, of course, the Israeli-Palestinian conflict—since this would require a willingness to show moral courage in facing the inevitable backlash within the U.S.

This faith and attitude is shared not just by neoconservatives and liberal hawks, but by a majority of the leaderships of both parties, by majorities in establishment think tanks like the Carnegie Endowment and the Brookings Institution and by much of the foreign policy bureaucracy. It is also not a fantasy cooked up by the neoconservatives, but has deep roots in certain strands of the American tradition. It is also often tragically mistaken.

The element of classical tragedy is that spreading democracy is a noble and worthwhile goal. A world in which democracies are more widespread, more secure, and more firmly anchored should indeed be part of the American legacy to humanity. The errors lie in believing that the spread of democracy consists of progress down a single known path to a fixed and preordained goal; that this progress can and should be linked to the achievement of short- and medium-term American foreign policy goals; that true democrats in other countries should be expected to invariably support those goals, even if they conflict with the national interests of their own countries; and that democracy can substitute for wise diplomacy.

Spreading American Righteousness

Insofar as this analysis is based on anything other than ideological faith, it draws almost exclusively on the history of Eastern Europe during and after the fall of Communism. But as Francis Fukuyama and others now have argued that the East European case is unique and must not be universalized. In Eastern Europe, nationalism was mobilized behind political and economic reform in a way that cannot be replicated else where—least of all in the Middle East, where much of Arab and Iranian nationalism is bitterly anti-American.

East Europeans committed themselves to democracy and reform as a way of escaping the hated influence of Moscow and fulfilling what they regard as their historically mandated national destinies of joining the West. In Eastern Europe, therefore, nationalism, a pro-American outlook and support for democracy all went together. Moreover, the push of nationalism in Eastern Europe was added to the tremendous pull of NATO [North Atlantic Treaty Organization] and European Union [E.U.] membership, and the assistance of European Union aid. But E.U. membership is assuredly not being offered to Egypt, Saudi Arabia or Iran.

In the Muslim world, both spreading democracy and attracting support for U.S. policies will be possible only if enough Muslims think that this is not only in their personal interest, but also in their patriotic interest. Preaching democracy and freedom at them is useless if they associate the adoption of Western-style democracy with national humiliation and the sacrifice of vital national interests.

The problem is that this democratist thinking is borne of an American culture that makes it very difficult for many Americans to understand other peoples' nationalisms. The tendency to conflate America, and American international interests, with righteousness can too easily lead to demonization of rival nations. This is especially true where these nations are ruled by non-democratic systems that Americans instinctively see as illegitimate. Many of the subjects of those states may share this feeling. On the other hand, on foreign and security issues, those states may well enjoy the support of the great majority of their peoples—at least when it comes to a defense of national interests and an angry rejection of foreign pressure. So dismissing the views of other states because those states are not democratic can therefore easily become a dismissal of the views of their peoples too, even when these views are expressed by such Westernized and liberal figures as the journalists of [Arab news sources] Al Jazeera and Al Arabiya.

Among neoconservatives and liberal hawks, the desire to spread democracy can also take a form explicitly dedicated to the weakening or even destruction of other states, even ones that are by no means fully-fledged enemies of the U.S. This kind of thinking has been given a tremendous impetus by the way in which mass "democratic" movements (which were, in fact, mostly nationalist) helped destroy the Soviet Union. Thus in a piece urging a tough U.S. strategy of confronting and weakening China, Max Boot of *The Wall Street Journal* wrote:

> Beyond containment, deterrence, and economic integration lies a strategy that the British never employed against either Germany or Japan—internal subversion. Sorry, the polite euphemisms are "democracy promotion" and "human rights protection," but these amount to the same thing: The freer China becomes, the less power the Communist oligarchy will enjoy. The United States should aim to "Taiwanize" the mainland—to spread democracy through such steps as increased radio broadcasts and Internet postings. . . . In general, the U.S. government should elevate the issue of human rights in our dealings with China. We need to champion Chinese dissidents, intellectuals, and political prisoners, and help make them as famous as Andrei Sakharov [Russian dissident], Václav Havel [president of the Czech Republic], and Lech Walesa [Polish union organizer and human rights activist].

Is it surprising that faced with these perspectives, not just the Communist regime but many ordinary Chinese and Russians view the U.S. preaching of democracy as part of a plan to weaken or even destroy their countries, irrespective of the cost to their populations?

The Myth of Democratic Peace

In terms of U.S. national interests, the argument for the spreading of democracy in the world is based on the idea of the "Democratic Peace": the belief, repeatedly stated by President [George W.] Bush and other officials, that "democracies don't fight other democracies." It is indeed true that established democracies don't fight each other, but only if other very important factors are either added to the equation or removed from it—which means this is not true as far as much of the world is concerned and for the foreseeable future.

Two elements must be present. First, there must be the legal and civil institutions that we in the West think of as naturally accompanying democracy, but are, in fact, absent from most quasi-democracies around the world. Second, a nation must have prosperity, which creates middle classes with a real commitment to democracy and spreads well-being through enough of the population that the masses accept being led by the middle classes rather than some variety of populist demagogue, as is increasingly the case in Latin America today.

The first element that has to be taken out of the mix—and cannot be—is nationalism, or some mixture of mutually hostile ethno-religious allegiances, as in Iraq. As Edward Mansfield and Jack Snyder have convincingly argued in their book "Electing to Fight" that new and weak democracies are, if anything, more likely to fight each other than established autocracies, as new freedom allows the public expression of long-suppressed national grievances which are then exploited by opportunist politicians. The fall of Communism led to a whole row of such cases in the Balkans and the Caucasus: The governments and movements which fought each other there in the 1990s were elected and mostly genuinely popular.

In the Middle East, we have already seen electoral victory for radical Islamist forces in Iran, the Shia areas of Lebanon, the Palestinian territories and the Pashtun areas of Pakistan.

To judge by recent limited elections in Saudi Arabia and Egypt, radicals would also win free votes there if the authorities permitted it.

In the long run, democracy is indeed necessary for progress and stability in the greater Middle East and for the defeat of terrorism and extremism. But moderate, nonaggressive, reasonably pro-Western democracies can only be established in the long run if the social, cultural and institutional foundations for them are laid by successful economic development— and this is a generational process. Furthermore, there is no chance of Arab democratic feeling developing in a moderate and pro-Western direction unless the U.S. changes many of its existing policies in the Middle East and shows a respect—a democratic respect—for the opinions of ordinary people in the region.

Democracy at the Expense of Freedom?

Even more strikingly, Washingtonian democratist orthodoxy presents an understanding of freedom that is very distorted from the one shared by most Americans and by the American tradition. The founding document on which the moral philosophy of America's approach to the world over the past 60 years is based is [U.S. president Franklin D.] Roosevelt's famous "Four Freedoms" speech of 1941, setting out the great principles which inspired the Western allies during the Second World War. Those who haven't read them often assume that they must include the freedom to vote. Wrong. The four freedoms are freedom of speech and expression, freedom of worship, freedom from want and freedom from fear. Democracy as such is nowhere mentioned.

Of course, none of these freedoms can exist under a totalitarian state but they can all exist under a moderately authoritarian one—as they did in several states of Europe before

1914. Freedom from want and freedom from fear both require states that respect their citizens, but are also strong enough to protect them.

Also required are the rule of law, a reasonably independent and efficient judiciary and police, a law-abiding, honest and rational bureaucracy and a population that enjoys basic rights of labor, movement and free discussion. All of these rights can and often have existed in countries where the executive has been unelected. None exist in rotten contemporary "democracies" like the Philippines. All of these things require that the state be strong enough to protect its citizens from outside aggression, internal rebellion, uncontrolled crime, and oppression and exploitation by predatory elites, including the state's servants acting on their own account and for their own profit, like the police in so many countries. Francis Lieber, adviser to President [Abraham] Lincoln, put it simply: "A weak government is a negation of liberty."

The need for a return to Roosevelt's "Four Freedoms" as a foundation for our thought about spreading freedom in the world is evident in the annual "Freedom in the World Survey" by the Congressionally-funded, semiofficial U.S. organization Freedom House. These documents are revered by much of the U.S. media and political establishment as holy writ, almost the U.S. equivalent of pronouncements by the Soviet Higher Party School. And like those pronouncements, many of Freedom House's ratings possess only a tangential relationship to reality.

What on earth, for example, are we to make of the fact that in 2006, Freedom House gave China its lowest mark, seven, for political freedom and a six for civil liberty—barely different from the seven and seven it gave in 1972, in the depth of the dreadful Cultural Revolution? Does Freedom House seriously think that ordinary Chinese are no freer today in real terms than at a time when their country was being swept by waves of monstrous totalitarian fanaticism, leading to the death, torture and deportation of tens of millions of people? Is this the same country of which two *New York Times* headlines of March 12 [2006] read, "A Sharp Debate Erupts in China Over Ideologies" and "Film in China: Fantasy trumps controversy, officially, but all movies are available one way or another." If challenged on this and similar idiocies, Freedom House officials tend to reply that they work on the basis of very narrow criteria, like free elections and private ownership of the media. But this is not an excuse—it is a confession.

Too much of the democratist ideology and its recommendations fail the test not just of study but of common sense, as well. Too many American democratists base their whole approach to the world on the assumption that they know how best to run countries of which they know nothing, whose languages they don't speak and which, quite often, they have never even visited! Would you hire a junior marketing executive with these credentials? For our part, we know perfectly well that we could not sell two plates of bean shoots in China or two sticks of kebab in Iran. We suspect, however, that most of those advocating democratism in these countries could not sell even half a plate.

The World Needs Better Governance, Not Democracy

Fareed Zakaria

Fareed Zakaria, the international editor of Newsweek, *has written for the* New York Times, New Yorker, New Republic, Wall Street Journal, *and the Web magazine* Slate. *In the following article, he argues that although the presidency of George W. Bush has focused on promoting democracy around the world, the president's actions and his administration's agenda have increasingly caused other countries to reject this system of government. Zakaria believes that an absence of governance and not an absence of democracy is the major problem faced by the world's developing nations. Instead of compensating countries for becoming democratic—no matter how corrupt, inefficient, and unfree they are in practice—the Bush administration should reward countries that improve human rights, reduce corruption, and increase their quality of governance.*

No [U.S.]president has attached his name more completely to the promotion of democracy than George W. Bush. He speaks of it with genuine passion and devoted virtually his entire second Inaugural to the subject. His administration talks constantly about its "freedom agenda" and interprets global events largely in such terms. Last summer [2006], for example, as missiles, car bombs and IEDs [improvised explosive devices] exploded across Lebanon, Gaza and Iraq, [U.S. secretary of state] Condoleezza Rice described the violence as the "birth pangs" of a new, democratic Middle East.

So it is striking to read this year's [2007] annual survey of "freedom in the world," released last week [mid-January 2007] by Freedom House, a nonprofit that is engaged in promoting

Fareed Zakaria, "The Limits of Democracy," *Newsweek*, January 29, 2007. www.newsweek.com. Reproduced by permission.

democracy around the globe. The report points out that 2006 was a bad year for liberty, under attack from creeping authoritarianism in Venezuela and Russia, a coup in Thailand, massive corruption in Africa and a host of more subtle reversals.

"The percentage of countries designated as free has failed to increase for nearly a decade and suggests that these trends may be contributing to a developing freedom stagnation," writes Freedom House director of research Arch Puddington in an essay released with the rankings.

Puddington also calls attention to the "pushback" against democracy. Regimes across the world are closing down nongovernmental organizations, newspapers and other groups that advocate for human rights. And, I would add, what is most striking is that these efforts are not being met with enormous criticism. Democracy proponents are on the defensive in many places.

What explains this paradox of freedom's retreat, even with a U.S. administration vociferous in promoting democracy? Some part of the explanation lies in the global antipathy to the U.S. president. "We have all been hurt by the association with the Bush administration," Saad Eddin Ibrahim, the Egyptian activist, told me last month. "Bush's arrogance has turned people off the idea of democracy," says Larry Diamond, co-editor of the *Journal of Democracy*.

But he goes on: "There's a lot more to it than that. We need to face up to the fact that in many developing countries democracy is not working very well." Diamond points to several countries where elections have been followed by governmental paralysis, corruption and ethnic warfare.

The poster child for this decline has to be Nigeria, a country often lauded for its democracy. In fact, the place is in free fall—an oil-rich country with per capita GDP [gross domestic product] down to $390 (from $1,000 20 years ago), a ranking below Bangladesh on the United Nations Human Development Index, and with a third of the country having placed itself under Sharia [Islamic law]. The new Freedom House survey rates Haiti higher now because it held elections last year [2006]. But does anyone believe that those polls will change the essential reality in Haiti—that it is a failed state?

The basic problem confronting the developing world today is not an absence of democracy but an absence of governance. From Iraq to the Palestinian territories to Nigeria to Haiti, this is the cancer that is eating away at the lives of people across the globe, plunging countries into chaos, putting citizens' lives and livelihoods at risk. It is what American foreign policy should be focused on. But the president's freedom agenda sees the entire complex process of political and economic development through one simple lens, which produces bad analysis and bad outcomes.

Consider Iraq. The administration has constantly argued that Iraq has witnessed amazing political progress over the last four years only to be undermined by violence. In fact, Iraq has seen its politics and institutions fall apart since the American invasion. Its state was dismantled, its economy disrupted, its social order overturned and its civic institutions and community corroded by sectarianism. Its three communities were never brought together to hammer out a basic deal on how they could live together. The only things that did take place in Iraq were elections (and the writing of a Constitution that is widely ignored). Those elections had wondrous aspects, but they also divided the country into three communities and hardened these splits. To describe the last four years as a period of political progress requires a strange definition of political development.

The administration now rewards democracies with aid. But why not have a more meaningful measure? Why not reward countries when they protect human rights, reduce corruption and increase the quality of governance?

"Our aid should be conditional on absolute standards," says Diamond. "The European Union has forced change on countries that want to join it by demanding real progress on tough issues."

An administration that thinks of itself as tough has been almost romantic in its views of the world. There is good and evil out there. But there is also competence and incompetence, and that makes a crucial difference around the globe—in fact, even in the United States.

Resisting Corporate Exploitation Through "Earth Democracy"

Vandana Shiva

Vandana Shiva, a physicist by training, is a spokesperson against the destructive effects of corporate control of land and resources. In the following article, Shiva describes the lives of the people of Nandigram, an agricultural community of Hindus and Muslims that has not been divided by communal forces or religious fundamentalism. She says that the Nandigram inhabitants' identity with the land, their earth identity, binds them together in a system she refers to as "Earth democracy," or "living democracy." Shiva compares Earth democracy to the destructive market-driven consumer democracy based on the Western model. Unlike market-driven democracy, which values development and profit, Earth democracy recognizes the value of all living systems upon which human welfare and survival wholly depend. Because of their system of social organization, their understanding of their environment, and their independence from powerful outside forces, the self-reliant people of Nandigram have been able to resist and defend their land and themselves.

Nandigram, a little known corner of Bengal, near the mouth of the Ganges river suddenly entered the nation's consciousness in early 2007.

The fertile land of Nandigram had been identified as a Special Economic Zone (Zone) [SEZ] for a chemical hub to be run by the Salim Group. The Salim group is named after its founder Liem Sior Liong, alias Sordono Salim. In 1965, when [second Indonesian president] Suharto overthrew [first Indonesian president] Saekarno, Salim emerged as a crony

Vandana Shiva, "Earth Democracy Thrives in Nandigram," *Z Magazine*, May 8, 2007. Reproduced by permission of the author.

who helped build Suharto's $16 billion assets. In the 1980's and 1990's during Indonesia's oil boom, Salim set up the Bank of Central Asia. He set up noodle, flour and bread businesses. He set up Indomobil Sukses International to make cars, Indo cement Tunggal Prakasa to make cement. Altogether he held 500 companies in Indonesia. This is the group that was trying to grab the land of farmers in Nandigram.

Nandigram was chosen because it is next to Haldia, a major port. SEZ's are tax free zones, where no law of the land applies—no environmental law, no labour law, no Panchayati Raj law for local governance. SEZ's were created in 2006 through the SEZ Act of 2005, which allowed the government to appropriate farmers' land and hand it over to corporations.

But the small and landless peasants of Nandigram stood up in revolt. They formed the Bhoomi Uched Pratirodh Samiti (the Movement against land grab) and refused to give up their land. In January, 2007 the first violence against the movement took place. On March 14th, 17 people were killed. On 29th April, another five lost their lives.

I was in Nandigram on 28th and 29th of April to pay homage to the martyrs of Nandigram and to work with the farmers to give them Navdanya seeds for setting up seed banks and starting organic farming. The farmers of Nandigram had succeeded in driving out Salim's chemical hub. I felt it was appropriate that we work together to make Nandigram a chemical free organic zone and the local communities were willing. All day we sat together and made plans while shootouts and bombing was taking place a few miles away. And during my visit to Nandigram I witnessed the practise of Earth Democracy in its most sophisticated form.

Nandigram's Living Economy

Nandigram is rich in soil, water and biodiversity, the real capital of communities. Each village has its ponds, making for water sovereignty. Each farm is a multifunctional production unit, producing "paan" [chew], coconut, rice, bananas, papaya, drumstick and the richest diversity of vegetables I have seen or tasted. In fact, during our meeting, the village square blossomed into a farmers market—with farmers selling four kinds of potatoes, eight kinds of bananas, gur (sugar) made from date palm and Palmyra palm.

Farmers markets like the one in Nandigram need no oil, no Walmart, no Reliance, no middlemen. Farmers are traders, sellers and the buyers. The market is self organised. The community organizes itself for trade. There is no Government license raj, no corporate control. This is the real free market, the real economic democracy.

The rich biodiversity of Nandigram supports a rich productivity. In conventional measurement, based on monocultures, industrial agriculture is presented as being more productive because inputs are not counted, nor is the destruction of biodiverse outputs and the soil, water and air. In a biodiversity assessment, the biodiversity dense small farms of Nandigram are much more productive than the most chemical and energy intensive industrial farms.

The lunch the community cooked for us was the most delicious food we have eaten—greens from the fields, dum-aloo made from indigenous potatoes, brinjal that melted in the mouth—and of course for the fish eaters the inevitable fish curry of Bengali cuisine. All other meals we had in Calcutta [India] or on the way to Nandigram in fancy restaurants were costly but inedible.

Nandigram has a food richness that big cities have lost. These are not impoverished, destitute communities but proud and self-reliant communities. In fact their self reliance was the ground of their resistance.

Nandigram is a post oil economy. Cycles, and cycle rickshaws are the main mode of transport. That is why when the Government unleashed violence against the people of Nandigram, they dug up the roads so no police or Government vehicle could enter. Their freedom from oil allowed them to defend their land freedom. Their living economy allowed them to have a living democracy. This is the practice of living economy, of [Indian spiritual leader Mohandas] Gandhi's "Swadesh".

Living Democracy

The living democracy in Nandigram allowed the communities to resist. Many farmers used to be members of CPM [Communist Party of India (Marxist)] but in their resistance to land they transcended party lines. The Land Sovereignty Movement in Nandgram is totally self organised. There has been an attempt to present the land conflict [as] a party conflict.

However, it is a conflict between global capital and local peasants, and the peasants have got organised because defending land is not a new issue in Nandigram. Peasants of the region participated in the revolt against East India Company [a trading company established by Great Britain] in 1857. Nandigram is a celebration of 150 years of India's first movement of independence from corporate rule with a new movement for freedom from corporate control. Nandigram was also the site of the Tebhaga Movement for Land Rights after the Great Bengal Famine. One can only enter Nandigram as a guest of the community—with their consent and their clearance. There is a high level of self-organisation, with women and children, old and young all involved in keeping watch for unwanted outsiders. Real democracy and living democracy, Gandhi's "Swaraj", is the capacity of self-organise.

Living Culture

The real strength of the people of Nandigram is their living culture—an agrarian culture, the culture of the land. This culture is common to the Hindus and the Muslims. Nandigram is strong because this community has not been divided by communal forces and the forces of religious fundamentalism. Hindus and Muslims practise their diverse faiths, but are part of one community. Even in the struggle against the SEZ and Salim, they have fought as one. Their identity with the land, their earth identity binds them together.

I have come away from Nandigram humbled and inspired. These are the elements of Earth Democracy we need to defend and protect from the violence and greed of corporate globalisation.

There Is No Such Thing as Islamic Democracy

David Bukay

David Bukay is a professor of Middle East studies at the University of Haifa in Israel. In the following article, he considers whether Islam and democracy are compatible. He says that several Muslim scholars, including John L. Esposito, argue that Islam enshrines democratic values. However, Bukay thinks such scholars twist the facts to suit their theories, the motive being to please Middle East audiences. This strategy, Bukay says, does little to solve the problem or the suspicions the West has about Islam and its modern adherents and political movements.

Some Western researchers support the Islamist claim that parliamentary democracy and representative elections are not only compatible with Islamic law, but that Islam actually encourages democracy. They do this in one of two ways: either they twist definitions to make them fit the apparatuses of Islamic government—terms such as democracy become relative—or they bend the reality of life in Muslim countries to fit their theories.

Western Apologia

Among the best known advocates of the idea that Islam both is compatible and encourages democracy is John L. Esposito, founding director of the Alwaleed bin Talal Center for Muslim-Christian Understanding at Georgetown University and the author or editor of more than thirty books about Islam and Islamist movements. Esposito and his various co-authors build their arguments upon tendentious assumptions and platitudes

David Bukay, "Can There Be an Islamic Democracy?" *Middle East Quarterly*, vol. 14, spring 2007, pp. 71–80. Copyright © 2007 Middle East Forum. Reproduced by permission.

such as "democracy has many and varied meanings;" "every culture will mold an independent model of democratic government;" and "there can develop a religious democracy."

He argues that "Islamic movements have internalized the democratic discourse through the concepts of shura [consultation], ijma' [consensus], and ijtihad [independent interpretive judgment]" and concludes that democracy already exists in the Muslim world, "whether the word democracy is used or not."

If Esposito's arguments are true, then why is democracy not readily apparent in the Middle East? Freedom House regularly ranks Arab countries as among the least democratic anywhere. Esposito adopts [political theorist Edward] Said's belief that Western scholarship and standards are inherently biased and lambastes both scholars who pass such judgments without experience with Islamic movements and those who have a "secular bias" toward Islam.

For example, in *Islam and Democracy* Esposito and co-author John Voll, associate director of the Prince Alwaleed Center, question Western attempts to monopolize the definition of democracy and suggest the very concept shifts meanings over time and place. They argue that every culture can mold an independent model of democratic government, which may or may not correlate to the Western liberal idea.

Only after eviscerating the meaning of democracy as the concept developed and derived from Plato and Aristotle in ancient Greece through Thomas Jefferson and James Madison in eighteenth century America, can Esposito and his fellow travelers advance theories of the compatibility of Islamism and democracy.

While Esposito's arguments may be popular within the Middle East Studies Association, democracy theorists tend to dismiss such relativism. Larry Diamond, co-editor of the *Journal of Democracy*, and Leonardo Morlino, a specialist in comparative politics at the University of Florence, ascribe seven features to any democracy: individual freedoms and civil liberties; rule of the law; sovereignty resting upon the people; equality of all citizens before the law; vertical and horizontal accountability for government officials; transparency of the ruling systems to the demands of the citizens; and equality of opportunity for citizens. This approach is important, since it emphasizes civil liberties, human rights and freedoms, instead of over-reliance on elections and the formal institutions of the state.

Esposito ignores this basic foundation of democracy and instead draws inspiration from men such as Indian philosopher Muhammad Iqbal (1877–1938), Sudanese religious leader Hasan al-Turabi (1932-), Iranian sociologist Ali Shariati (1933–77), and former Iranian president Muhammad Khatami (1943–), who argue that Islam provides a framework for combining democracy with spirituality to remedy the alleged spiritual vacuum in Western democracies. They endorse Khatami's view that democracies need not follow a formula and can function not only in a liberal system but also in socialist or religious systems; they adopt the important twentieth century Indian (and, later, Pakistani) exegete Abu al-A'la al-Mawdudi's concept of a "theo-democracy," in which three principles: tawhid (unity of God), risala (prophethood) and khilafa (caliphate) underlie the Islamic political system.

But Mawdudi argues that any Islamic polity has to accept the supremacy of Islamic law over all aspects of political and religious life—hardly a democratic concept, given that Islamic law does not provide for equality of all citizens under the law regardless of religion and gender. Such a formulation also denies citizens a basic right to decide their laws, a fundamental concept of democracy. Although he uses the phrase theo-democracy to suggest that Islam encompassed some democratic principles, Mawdudi himself asserted Islamic democracy to be a self-contradiction: the sovereignty of God and sovereignty of the people are mutually exclusive. An Islamic democracy would be the antithesis of secular Western democracy.

Esposito and Voll respond by saying that Mawdudi and his contemporaries did not so much reject democracy as frame it under the concept of God's unity. Theo-democracy need not mean a dictatorship of state, they argue, but rather could include joint sovereignty by all Muslims, including ordinary citizens. Esposito goes even further, arguing that Mawdudi's Islamist system could be democratic even if it eschews popular sovereignty, so long as it permits consultative assemblies subordinate to Islamic law.

While Esposito and Voll argue that Islamic democracy rests upon concepts of consultation (shura), consensus (ijma'), and independent interpretive judgment (ijtihad), other Muslim exegetes [critical interpreters] add hakmiya (sovereignty). To support such a conception of Islamic democracy, Esposito and Voll rely on Muhammad Hamidullah (1908–2002), an Indian Sufi scholar of Islam and international law; Ayatollah Baqir as-Sadr (1935–80), an Iraqi Shi'ite cleric; Muhammad Iqbal (1877–1938), an Indian Muslim poet, philosopher and politician; Khurshid Ahmad, a vice president of the Jama'at-e-lslami of Pakistan; and Taha al-Alwani, an Iraqi scholar of Islamic jurisprudence. The inclusion of Alwani underscores the fallacy of Esposito's theories. In 2003, the FBI [Federal Bureau of Investigation] identified Alwani as an unindicted co-conspirator in a trial of suspected Palestinian Islamic Jihad leaders and financiers.

Just as Esposito eviscerates the meaning of democracy to enable his thesis, so, too, does he twist Islamic concepts. Shura is an advisory council, not a participatory one. It is a legacy of tribalism, not sovereignty. Nor does ijma' express the consensus of the community at large but rather only the elders and established leaders. As for independent judgment, many Sunni scholars deem ijtihad closed in the eleventh century.

The Argument of Compatibility

Esposito's arguments have not only permeated the Middle Eastern studies academic community but also gained traction with public intellectuals through books written by journalists and policy practitioners.

In both journal articles and book length works as well as in underlying assumptions within her reporting, former *Los Angeles Times* and current *Washington Post* diplomatic correspondent Robin Wright argues that Islamism could transform into more democratic forms. In 2000, for example, she argued in *The Last Great Revolution* that a profound transformation was underway in Iran in which pragmatism replaced revolutionary values, arrogance had given way to realism, and the "government of God" was ceding to secular statecraft. Far from becoming more democratic, though, the supreme leader and Revolutionary Guards consolidated control; freedoms remain elusive, political prisoners incarcerated, and democracy imaginary.

Underlying Wright's work is the idea that neither Islam nor Muslim culture is a major obstacle to political modernity. She accepts both the Esposito school's arguments that shura, ijma', and ijtihad form a basis on which to make Islam compatible with political pluralism. She shares John Voll's belief that Islam is an integral part of the modern world, and she says the central drama of reform is the attempt to reconcile Islam and modernity by creating a worldview compatible with both.

In her article "Islam and Liberal Democracy," she profiles two prominent Islamist thinkers, Rachid al-Ghannouchi, the exiled leader of Tunisia's Hizb al-Nahda (Renaissance Party), and Iranian philosopher and analytical chemist Abdul-Karim Soroush. While she argues that their ideas represent a realistic confluence of Islam and democracy, she neither defines democracy nor treats her cases' studies with a dispassionate eye. Ghannouchi uses democratic terms without accepting them let alone understanding their meaning. He remains not a modernist but an unapologetic Islamist.

Wright ignores that Soroush led the purge of liberal intellectuals from Iranian universities in the wake of the Islamic Revolution. While Soroush spoke of civil rights and tolerance, he applied such privileges only to those subscribing to Islamic democracy. He also argued that although Islam means "submission," there is no contradiction to the freedoms inherent in democracy. Islam and democracy are not only compatible but their association inevitable. In a Muslim society, one without the other is imperfect. He argues that the will of the majority shapes the ideal Islamic state. But, in practice, this does not occur. As in Iran, many Islamists constrain democratic processes and crush civil society. Those with guns, not numbers, shape the state. Among Arab-Islamic states, there are only authoritarian regimes and patrimonial leadership; the jury is still out on whether Iraq can be a stable exception. Soroush, however, contradicts himself: Although Islam should be an open religion, it must retain its essence. His argument that Islamic law is expandable would be considered blasphemous by many contemporaries who argue that certain principles within Islamic law are immutable. Upon falling out of favor with revolutionary authorities in Iran, he fled to the West. Sometimes, academics only face the fallacy of what sounds plausible in the ivy tower when events force them to face reality.

What Ghannouchi and Soroush have in common, and what remains true with any number of other Islamist officials, is that, regardless of rhetoric, they do not wish to reconcile Islam and modernity but to change the political order. It is easier to adopt the rhetoric of democracy than its principles.

While time has proven Wright wrong, the persistence of Esposito exegetes remains. Every few years, a new face emerges to revive old arguments. The most recent addition is Noah Feldman, a frequent media commentator and Arabic-speaking law professor at Harvard University. In 2003, Feldman published *After Jihad: America and the Struggle for Islamic Democracy*, which explores the prospects for democracy in the Islamic world. His thesis rehashes Esposito's 1992 book *The Islamic Threat: Myth or Reality?* and the 1996 Esposito-Voll collaboration *Islam and Democracy*. Even after the 9-11 [September 11, 2001] terrorist attacks, Feldman argues that the age of violent jihad is past, and Islamism is evolving in new, more peaceful, and democratic directions. Included in Feldman's list of Islamic democrats is Yusuf al-Qaradawi, an Islamist theoretician who has endorsed suicide bombing and the murder of homosexuals.

While most academic debates do not exit the classroom, the debate over the compatibility of Islam and democracy affects policy. Feldman pushes the conclusion that the Islamist threat is illusionary. Accordingly, he argues that Islamist movements should have a chance to govern. Feldman concludes with the prescription that U.S. policymakers should adopt an inclusive attitude toward political Islam. "An established religion that does not coerce religious belief and that treats religious minorities as equals may be perfectly compatible with democracy," he explained in a September 2003 interview.

Shireen Hunter, a former Iranian diplomat who now directs the Islam program at the Center for Strategic and International Studies, also repackages Esposito's general arguments in her book, *The Future of Islam and the West: Clash of Civilizations or Peaceful Coexistence?*, and, more recently, in *Modernization, Democracy, and Islam*, her edited collection with Huma Malik, the assistant director of Esposito's Prince Alwaleed Bin Talal Center for Muslim-Christian Understanding at Georgetown University. Both books deny the Islamist threat and try to reconcile Islamic teaching with Western values. She seeks to counter Samuel Huntington's *Clash of Civilization* and gives an assessment of the relative role of both conflictual and cooperate factors of Muslim-Western relations. She argues that the fusion of the spiritual and the temporal in Islam is no greater than in other religions. Therefore, the slower pace of democratization in Muslim countries cannot be attributed to Islam itself. Although Hunter acknowledges that Muslim countries have a poor record of modernization and democracy, she blames external factors such as colonialism and the international economic system.

Other scholars take obsequiousness to new levels. Anna Jordan, who gives no information about her expertise but is widely published on Islamist Internet sites, argues that the Qur'an supports the principles of Western democracy as they are defined by William Ebenstein and Edwin Fogelman, two professors of political science who focus on the ideas and ideologies that define democracy. By utilizing various Qur'anic verses, Jordan finds that the Islamic holy book supports rational empiricism and individual rights, rejects the state as the ultimate authority, promotes the freedom to associate with any religious group, accepts the idea that the state is subordinate to law, and accepts due process and basic equality.

Most of her citations, though, do not support her conclusions and, in some cases, suggest the opposite. Rather than support the idea of "rational empiricism," for example, Sura 17:36 mandates complete submission to the authority of God. Other citations are irrelevant in context and substance to her arguments. Her assertion that the Qur'an assures the "basic equality of all human beings" rests upon verses commanding equality among Muslims and Muslims only, plus a verse warning against schisms among Muslims.

Gudrun Kramer, chair of the Institute of Islamic Studies at the Free University in Berlin [Germany], also accepts the Esposito thesis. She writes that the central stream in Islam "has come to accept crucial elements of political democracy: pluralism, political participation, governmental accountability, the rule of law, and the protection of human rights." In her opinion, the Muslim approach to human rights and freedom is more advanced than many Westerners acknowledge.

Islamist Rejection of the Compatibility Theory

Ironically, while Western scholars perform intellectual somersaults to demonstrate the compatibility of Islam and democracy, prominent Muslim scholars argue democracy to be incompatible with their religion. They base their conclusion on two foundations: first, the conviction that Islamic law regulates the believer's activities in every area of life, and second, that the Muslim society of believers will attain all its goals only if the believers walk in the path of God. In addition, some Muslim scholars further reject anything that does not have its origins in the Qur'an.

Hasan al-Banna (1906–49), the founder of the Muslim Brotherhood, sought to purge Western influences. He taught that Islam was the only solution and that democracy amounted to infidelity to Islam. Sayyid Qutb (1906–66), the leading theoretician of the Muslim Brotherhood, objected to the idea of popular sovereignty altogether. He believed that the Islamic state must be based upon the Qur'an, which he argued provided a complete and moral system in need of no further legislation. Consultation—in the traditional Islamic sense rather than in the manner of Esposito's extrapolations—was sufficient.

Mawdudi, while used by Esposito, argued that Islam was the antithesis of any secular Western democracy that based sovereignty upon the people and rejected the basics of Western democracy. More recent Islamists such as Qaradawi argue that democracy must be subordinate to the acceptance of God as the basis of sovereignty. Democratic elections are therefore heresy, and since religion makes law, there is no need for legislative bodies. Outlining his plans to establish an Islamic state in Indonesia, Abu Bakar Bashir, a Muslim cleric and the leader of the Indonesian Mujahideen Council, attacked democracy and the West and called on Muslims to wage jihad against the ruling regimes in the Muslim world. "It is not democracy that we want, but Allah-cracy," he explained.

Nor does acceptance of basic Western structures imply democracy. Under Ayatollah Ruhollah Khomeini, the Islamic Republic adopted both a constitution and a parliament, but their existence did not make Iran more democratic. Indeed, Khomeini continued to wield supreme power and formed a number of bodies—the revolutionary foundations, for example—which remained above constitutional law.

Is Islamic Democracy Possible?

The Islamic world is not ready to absorb the basic values of modernism and democracy. Leadership remains the prerogative of the ruling elite. Arab and Islamic leadership are patrimonial, coercive, and authoritarian. Such basic principles as sovereignty, legitimacy, political participation and pluralism, and those individual rights and freedoms inherent in democracy do not exist in a system where Islam is the ultimate source of law.

The failure of democracies to take hold in Gaza and Iraq justify both the 1984 declaration by Samuel P. Huntington and the argument a decade later by Gilles Kepel, a prominent French scholar and analyst of radical Islam, that Islamic cultural traditions may prevent democratic development.

Emeritus Princeton historian Bernard Lewis is also correct in explaining that the term democracy is often misused. It has turned up in surprising places—the Spain of General [Francisco] Franco, the Greece of the colonels, the Pakistan of the generals, the Eastern Europe of the commissars—usually prefaced by some qualifying adjective such as "guided," "basic," "organic," "popular," or the like, which serves to dilute, deflect, or even reverse the meaning of the word.

Islam may be compatible with democracy, but it depends on what is understood as Islam. This is not universally agreed on and is based on a hope, not on reality. Both Turkey and the West African country of Mali are democracies even though the vast majority of their citizens are Muslim. But, the political Islam espoused by the Muslim Brotherhood and other Islamists is incompatible with liberal democracy.

Furthermore, if language has an impact on thinking, then the Middle East will achieve democracy only slowly, if at all. In traditional Arabic, Persian, and Turkish, there is no word for "citizen." Rather, older texts use cognates—in Arabic, muwatin; in Turkish, vatandaslik; in Persian, sharunad—respectively, closer in meaning to the English "compatriot" or "countryman." The Arabic and Turkish come from watan, meaning "country." Muwatin is a neologism and while it suggests progress, the Western concept of freedom—understood as the ability to participate in the formation, conduct, and lawful removal and replacement of government—remains alien in much of the region.

Islamists themselves regard liberal democracy with contempt. They are willing to accommodate it as an avenue to power but as an avenue that runs only one way. Hisham Sharabi (1927–2005), the influential Palestinian scholar and political activist, has said that Islamic fundamentalism expresses mass sentiment and belief as no nationalist or socialist (and we may add democratic) ideology has been able to do up until now.

Why Are So Many Scholars Interested in Linking Islam with Democracy?

Why then are so many Western scholars keen to show the compatibility between Islamism and democracy? The popularity of post-colonialism and post-modernism within the academy inclines intellectuals to accommodate Islamism. Political correctness inhibits many from addressing the negative phenomenon in foreign cultures. It is considered laudable to prove the compatibility of Islam and democracy; it is labeled

"Islamophobic" or racist to suggest incompatibility or to differentiate between positive and negative interpretations of Islam.

Many policymakers are also conflict-adverse. Islamists exploit the Western cultural desire to accommodate while Western thinkers and policymakers attempt to ameliorate differences by seeking to find common ground in definitions if not reality.

Into the mix comes Islamist propaganda, portraying Islam as peace-loving, embracing of civil rights and, even in its less tolerant forms, compatible with all democratic values. The problem is that the free world ignores the possibility that political Islam can threaten democracy not only in Middle Eastern societies but also in the West. The legitimization of political Islam has lent democratic respectability to an ideology and political system at odds with the basic tenets of democracy.

Esposito's statement that "the United States must restrain its one-dimensional attitude to democracy and recognize [that] the authentic roots of democracy exist in Islam" shows a basic ignorance of both democracy and Islamist teachings. These conclusions are exacerbated when Esposito places blame for the aggressiveness and terrorism of Islamic fundamentalism on the West and on Said's "Orientalists." It is one thing to be wrong in the classroom, but it can be far more dangerous when such wrong-headed theories begin to affect policy.

Critiques of Democracy

Chapter Preface

From ancient times, democracy has had its champions and detractors. One of the harshest critics of Athenian democracy was the philosopher Plato, who charged that such a system of government inevitably leads to "mob rule," with those in power pandering to "pleasure-seekers" concerned mainly with satisfying their base desires. He argued too that democracy fosters disagreement and conflict and leads to rule by men who might be great orators that can sway the masses but who have no true governing skills. There can be no stability in a polity, Plato believed, unless order is established and the state is led by "philosopher-kings," those who are naturally wise, intelligent, rational, self-controlled, and suited to make decisions for the benefit of all.

Other critics of democracy have also held that democracy leads to chaos. British statesman Edmund Burke, writing after the bloody events of the French Revolution, decried the "blind, ferocious democracy" that sought to destroy all order and tradition. Although Burke was a champion of liberty and sought in his career to prevent abuses of monarchical control, he believed the rule of a king was preferable to the "tyranny of the majority" that was inevitable in democratic rule. It is important to remember that Burke, like Plato, was criticizing "direct democracy," which is different from liberal democracy with its constitutional checks and balances that protect the rights of individuals in the minority. Modern libertarians also warn against the dangers of a democracy without the safeguards of constitutional liberalism, which endangers fundamental rights.

Anarchists—those who rebel against authority, order, or a ruling party—also criticize democracy for not allowing human freedom to flourish. The Italian anarchist Errico Malatesta maintained that democracy is in fact a lie, and that what is commonly viewed as democracy is oligarchy—power in the hands of only a few. He argued that representative democracy, even with constitutionally established checks, is open to abuse and the people's opinions are largely unrepresented. Only anarchy, he believes, can ensure freedom for all. Socialists have also argued that what passes for democracy does not reflect the general will of the people but the interests of elites, leaving citizens with no actual power over their political lives.

In the early twenty-first century, even as much of the world has accepted democracy as the most favorable form of government, democracy has been the subject of considerable censure. Much of the recent criticism of democracy has come from those who see deep flaws in the way that democracy has come to be viewed and promoted in the world. The neoliberal economic model of democracy, in which the free market is upheld as a central value, has come under attack by some feminists who see it as degrading the economic and social lives of most of the world's inhabitants. Some thinkers in the Muslim world argue that the inconsistencies of Western governments regarding the rights of those who do not share their values make the rest of the world suspicious of democracy. In a world in which democracy is heavily touted as the cure-all to global ills, a better understanding of the concept is needed and more consistency is essential when applying its principles, say these critics, otherwise democracy will be seen as an empty idea. Or even worse, it could be manipulated by the powerful and turned into tyranny—exactly what democracy was designed to protect against.

An Islamic Critique of the Western Democratic Model

Mohamed Elhachmi Hamdi

Mohamed Elhachmi Hamdi is a Tunisian-born writer. He is the founder and editor-in-chief of the Arabic-language newspaper Al Mustakillah *and the English and Arabic quarterly* The Diplomat. *He was a member of the Tunisian Islamic movement al-Nahda for more than ten years before his resignation in 1992. In the following article, Hamdi says that the inconsistencies of Western governments make the rest of the world suspicious of democracy. He contends that the perception in the Middle East of Western democracy is that it is morally hollow even while it preaches to the rest of the world. He criticizes scholars as well who view "Islamic reformists" who echo Western values as somehow the salvation of the Middle East. The Middle East, Hamdi says, can learn from Westerners about democracy, but it must be done in a spirit of dialogue and not with an attitude of cultural and moral arrogance and superiority.*

[Journalist] Robin Wright and [writer and professor] Bernard Lewis have a number of sensible and positive things to say about what might be called the "democratic credentials" of Islam. To their credit, both seem to recognize that Islam is not necessarily opposed to representative and accountable government. I begin with these words of praise in order to situate my criticism of their essays in its proper context. My goal is not to diminish their work, but to broaden understanding between Muslims and non-Muslims, especially the non-Muslims of the West.

While Wright does not define democracy, Lewis pithily describes it as "a polity where the government can be changed

Mohamed Elhachmi Hamdi, "Islam and Liberal Democracy: The Limits of the Western Model," *Journal of Democracy*, vol. 7, no. 2, 1996, pp. 81–85. Copyright © 1996 **The Johns Hopkins University Press.** Reproduced by permission.

by elections as opposed to one where elections are changed by the government." I accept this definition without reservation. The problem is that Westerners tend to associate this definition with their own model of democracy, which is difficult to accept universally. It is often deemed dangerous to question Western democracy for fear of being labeled an antidemocrat; still, at least half of the world's population does not adhere to this democratic model. Is it unreasonable to wonder if this suggests problems with the Western model itself?

Western intellectuals should take more seriously than they do the possibility that there are limitations to their brand of democracy. Consider the ever-increasing role that money plays in determining who can run for public office in the United States, let alone who can win. Money is so important in U.S. politics that it may in fact have more influence than the people themselves in choosing those who govern. Or consider in how many countries Western democracy has failed to prevent racism toward blacks, or anti-Semitism. Anti-Semitism, in fact, is a European product that could never have come about in the Islamic world, which is built on belief in the three main messengers of divine revelation—Moses, Jesus, and Mohammed, peace be upon them.

Although most Western writers speak of democracy as a universal set of values, Western deeds tell a very different story. The French, for instance, behave democratically in France itself, but not in Algeria, where they have committed some of this blood-drenched century's most horrific atrocities. This has also been the case with the U.S. government's policies in parts of Central America and the Muslim world.

Nor are Western inconsistencies all that dampen the Western democratic model's appeal. Not all societies stand to benefit from a multiparty system, for in some circumstances such pluralism might only serve to deepen existing tribal or sectarian divisions (Rwanda, the Sudan, Liberia, and even Lebanon come to mind). It is also questionable whether the rule of 51 percent is a workable solution for many African and Asian societies, which need the efforts of all political groups, not only the one that gains victory in an election.

On certain moral questions, moreover, Western democracy appears—not just to outside critics but to many Westerners—to be running amok. It is hard to see why lax Western mores that weaken or destroy the family—that most crucial of all social institutions—should be exported to the rest of the world under the banner of democracy. Indeed, I cannot foresee any Islamic country under any circumstances accepting certain social practices that until recently were not generally accepted in the West either, but have now become common there.

There is no chance for a constructive dialogue among cultures and civilizations as long as those who dominate public discourse in the West continue to see themselves as the upholders of political and moral standards for the entire world. Unfortunately, a bit of this self-satisfaction is discernible in the way in which Wright and Lewis insist on comparing tendencies of thought in the Islamic world today to the Reformation in Christian Europe five centuries ago. This fails to account for the huge differences in concepts and movements, and drives home the point that only by seeing the limitations of their own standards can Westerners look more positively and objectively at the histories and cultures of other peoples.

A Voice or an Echo?

Five years ago [in 1991] in Washington, D.C., I translated while Robin Wright interviewed Rachid al-Ghannouchi about his views on the West in general and democracy in particular. I remember how impressed she was by his liberal views, and thus was not surprised to read her praise for him as an Islamic reformist. Wright is an intelligent and hard-working journalist, unaffected by negative Western stereotypes concerning Arabs or Muslims.

There is a problem, however: Wright is mostly interested in Muslims who, in effect, speak her mind back to her in terms that she finds familiar, and who reassure her of the supremacy of her own Western values. Ghannouchi fits this role perfectly. As an exiled politician seeking support from Western circles against the regime that he wants to replace in Tunisia, his strategy has been to play the "democracy card." This is why he is one of the favorite Arab Islamists of Wright and others, such as Professor John Esposito of the United States and François Burgat of France. Westerners have not exactly been keen to engage in direct dialogue with the most prominent representatives of "Islamic fundamentalism" from Iran, Egypt, or the Sudan. Ghannouchi has held up a comforting mirror to the West amid what is generally seen as a dangerous field. Thus Wright and those like her have been ready to disregard those words and deeds of Ghannouchi's—and there are many—that clearly contradict his democratic rhetoric.

To present the West with a congenially "Westernized" version of Islam, whether for political or other reasons, has been a particular ambition of certain Islamic thinkers for the last two centuries. Albert Hourani summed it up neatly when he described the efforts of the famous Egyptian scholar and imam of the al-Azhar mosque, Mohamed Abduh (1849–1905):

> He carried farther a process we have already seen at work in the thought of Tahtawi, Khair al-Din, and al-Afghani: that of identifying certain traditional concepts of Islamic thought with the dominant ideas of modern Europe. In this line of thought *maslaha* gradually turns into utility, *shura* into parliamentary democracy, *ijma* into public opinion; Islam itself becomes identical with civilisation and activity, the norms of the nineteenth-century social thought. It was of course easy in this way to distort if not destroy the precise meaning of the Islamic concepts, to lose that which distinguished Islam from other religions and even from nonreligious humanism.

Abduh was widely recognized as a scholar and thinker; Ghannouchi is primarily a politician who has different audiences to please, both inside and outside his party. Many of his critics think that he has failed to be coherent in his views on many important issues, including his stance toward the West, the way in which to change the Tunisian regime, the status of women, and democracy itself. For them, this raises a huge question about the validity and sincerity of the "liberal" views that Robin Wright extols.

Concerning the "Christian Illness"

Bernard Lewis's essay, too, reflects the desire of many Westerners to praise whoever follows their preferred path. Perhaps that is why he overlooks the Egyptian regime's abysmal human rights record and rampant corruption in order to cite Egypt as one of the foremost Islamic countries to be "taking significant steps toward modernization and democratization."

What most requires clarification is Lewis's view that "it may be that Muslims, having contracted a Christian illness, will consider a Christian remedy, that is to say, the separation of religion and the state." There is nothing new about this "remedy," which is one that the West has tried before to impose on Islamic countries, albeit without major success. The heart of the matter is that no Islamic state can be legitimate in the eyes of its subjects without obeying the main teachings of the *shari'a* [Islamic law based on the Muslim holy book, the Koran]. A secular government might coerce obedience, but Muslims will not abandon their belief that state affairs should be supervised by the just teachings of the holy law. This is not to recommend autocracy, but to say that Islam should be the main frame of reference for the constitution and laws of predominantly Muslim countries. Even in the United States and Europe, there are supreme values that are embodied in the constitutions and the laws of those lands. Islam has been playing this role for the last 1,400 years, mostly for the good of

Muslims, and there is no need to replace it with a set of Western values. As both Wright and Lewis mention, Islamic teachings condemn tyranny and corruption: these teachings always have been, are now, and always will be a beacon and a refuge for those oppressed by unjust rulers or invaders.

Why on earth should all the world convert to Western norms? Would it not be better to preserve a fruitful pluralism in the world, by which nations can express themselves in different ways, while respecting the basic values that are essential for all human beings?

The only way that secularism can be kept alive in the Islamic world is by local Muslim dictatorships, supported by Western power. Lewis is wrong to claim that most Islamic countries have gained independence from Western forces, and that their misfortunes on the road to democracy have been the result of their own mistakes. Every objective observer would admit that the West is still very much involved in the day-to-day affairs of most Muslim countries, especially those in the Arab world. This involvement takes the sad form of an unholy alliance with corrupt, isolated elites who do not respect democracy in *any* form, Western or otherwise. What keeps all too many regimes in power in the Arab world is not their own legitimacy, but rather control over the armed forces and support from the Western nations whose interests they serve.

Here we see the true face of secularism in most of the Islamic world: a new form of submission to the same old colonial powers. These powers may have democratic polities, but it is democracy meant for Westerners only, and does not imply any moral duties toward other nations. Useful antidemocrats in the Muslim, and especially the Arab, world easily gain Western help. Ordinary Arabs know this, which is why they stand ready to support whoever raises the flag of true independence, including the Islamists of Turkey, Algeria, Egypt, the Sudan, and Iran.

Of course, secularism is not the only obstacle confronting the cause of political liberty in the Islamic world. We had our own problems even before being dominated by the West. Islam may have been misused and may continue to be misused by corrupt and tyrannical rulers intent on legitimizing their policies by giving them what appears to be religious sanction. Here, indeed, lies one of the most formidable challenges facing contemporary Islamic thought as it strives to outline a regime that is Islamic but also representative and accountable. There is no doubt that we can benefit from the rich experience of Western democracy. I will go further: we Muslims not only can, but *must* learn from the West if we are to overcome the many problems prevalent in the Islamic world. But for this to be possible we need a dialogue between peoples in which the respective identities and interests of each are accorded equal respect. Muslims know this well, and are ready to extend the hand of respect to their Western counterparts. The question is: Are those in the West ready to do the same for Muslims?

A Socialist Critique
of Democracy

Michael Levin

Michael Levin teaches political theory at Goldsmiths College, University of London. In the following review of Takis Fotopoulos's Towards An Inclusive Democracy, *Levin discusses the main theoretical, tactical, and strategic issues that the conception of "inclusive democracy" gives rise to. He explains that inclusive democracy is derived from a synthesis of two major historical traditions: the classical democratic and the socialist. Fotopoulos, explains Levin, views the current practice of democracy in the United States as having been undermined by globalization. The present order is unsustainable, he says, and must be extended to include social, economic, and ecological democracy as well.*

Do we not all take democracy seriously? It is, after all, the badge we pin on ourselves, the status symbol that we take to elevate our country above others that don't manage it so well. And the last decades have been a successful time for democracy. We have witnessed the fall of communism, the defeat of apartheid and the end of the military régimes in South America. The key-statement for the initial phase of self-congratulation was Francis Fukuyama's *The End of History and the Last Man*

Takis Fotopoulos's very first sentence puts Fukuyama in his place: The collapse of 'actually existing socialism' does not reflect the 'triumph of capitalism', as celebrated by its ideologues. However, the democracy that 'we' celebrate can more precisely be designated as liberal democracy, that is democracy

Michael Levin, "Still Taking Democracy Seriously," *The International Journal of INCLUSIVE DEMOCRACY*, vol. 1, May, 2005. Reproduced by permission. www.inclusive democracy.org/journal.

within a capitalist framework. Here, with one person one vote, we are all equal on our occasional visits to the polling-booth but in no other respect.

To defenders of liberal democracy this is adequate. Hayek was keen to point out that democracy refers only to a type of government and so has no application to other organisations. This is in contrast to the designation given by Alexis de Tocqueville just over a century and a half ago. For Tocqueville political democracy was merely one aspect of a wider phenomenon. Democracy as a whole was the leveling process that had, over centuries, worn down the hierarchical aristocratic gradations so enjoyed by his own forebears. Tocqueville described this process as inevitable, yet simultaneously warned of the emergence of an aristocracy of manufacturers, a class that might acquire powers equal to those of the displaced landed aristocracy but was unlikely to match their sense of social responsibility. Do we not, in this sub-theme, find a presentiment of our situation?

Political Equalities, Economic Disparities

What we have reached might be described as the paradox of liberal democracy—that the parts are in contradiction, for how can we be equal politically when we are so unequal economically? Consider the case of the current British Labour government, swept to power in 1997 by a wave of popular enthusiasm. Do those of you who voted for it have the same degree of influence on it as Bernie Ecclestone of Formula One [racing] fame, or of Rupert Murdoch, the Australian-American newspaper magnate? These cases remind one of [Scottish philosopher] James Mill's dictum 'that the business of government is properly the business of the rich; and that they will always obtain it, either by bad means, or good.'

Socialism vs. Social Democracy

Of course, it was precisely this situation that socialism emerged to overcome. However, to cut a long story short, the current tendency is to regard socialism as discredited. Its communist variant has fallen in the Soviet Union and Eastern Europe. Its remaining outposts in China and East Asia are unlikely to be extended. The notion that communism might introduce or deepen democracy proved an illusion of their initial phase of power. The Leninist idea of the Soviet as a higher form of democracy disintegrated into the Stalinist one-party state.

Western Social Democracy, however, never sought to challenge parliamentary democracy. When in power the rights of other parties and the freedoms of association and of the press were never threatened. Social Democracy has to its credit a significant democratic achievement for through its impetus the class disqualification to political participation was overcome and, in its best phase, it sought to obtain both full employment and adequate welfare provision.

However, beyond that the democratic thrust of Social Democracy was thwarted, both by its Fabian managerialism and by the society's capitalist framework. Throughout the 1970s those on the left subjected social democracy to a withering critique that may, partially and ironically, have led to a toss of self-confidence that, in combination with other factors, facilitated its downfall and replacement by the New Right. However, as [folk singer] Bob Dylan so memorably put it 'the wheel's still in spin' and Social Democracy re-emerged in the late 1990s into a brief period of unparalleled dominance in European governments. However, although it still bears the label, it was not the Social Democracy that we knew before. Fotopoulos reminds us that as 'these parties ... bear almost no relation at all to the traditional social-democratic parties of the 1950–75 period, they should more accurately be called "social liberal" rather than social-democratic parties.'

Social Democracy's opportunity has come both through a withdrawal of support from the full New Right doctrine and from the fact that it can no longer be feared as an agent of Soviet power. However, liberation from that context has been countered by at least two disadvantages. Firstly, the reduced preponderance of the industrial working class has increased Social Democracy's need to appeal to the middle classes. Secondly, the power of the state has been reduced by further globalization and so governments now have less control of economic management.

The Negative Influence of Capitalism

This is the logical starting-point of Fotopoulos's book. In one sense it belongs to the genre of pre-Thatcherite [before the era of British prime minister Margaret Thatcher] critiques of Social Democracy in that it seeks to analyse its failings and find a way of overcoming them. It is, then, an updating of that debate for it commences with a thorough analysis of the significantly changed current situation. Its point of continuity with earlier debate is that it takes the bold and currently unpopular view that the socialist project is still a plausible one. Fotopoulos, then, is not among those on the left who have collapsed into the individualist paradise of post-modernism. Nor is he among those who call on Social Democracy to return to its traditional path. 'Social democracy . . . is dead', he tells us in the book's very first paragraph. It has been undermined by globalization and the consequent decline of the state, which was the prime site of Social Democratic activity. At one time the United States of America was considered exceptional amongst modern industrial societies in that the land without socialism was simultaneously, or one might say consequently, the land with poor welfare provision, weak trade unions and a particularly deep divide between rich and poor. What should have been a warning to other countries seems instead to have become a model. Fotopoulos notes 'the "Americanization" of the political process all over the advanced capitalist world'. We thus join the USA in, if not 'The End of Ideology', then the end of ideological competition. If the loss of old Social Democracy and the decline of state welfarism produces, among other things, a narrowing of the political spectrum, then we simultaneously impoverish both the needy and our liberal democratic system. Old Social Democracy, as should now be clear, is no longer a plausible option. It emerged at a time when ecological concerns had no impact. However much might divide capitalism from socialism both shared a 'growth ideology' as their 'ultimate ideological foundation'. Furthermore, global capital now dominates global labour. The state is caught in the middle between international economic power on the one side and, on the other, the real communities where people live and work. Fotopoulos's project is to recommend that the latter reclaim the power that has been usurped by the former.

The Project to Reclaim Social Democracy

Fukuyama thought that we were there. For him there was no further project. This is it. Not, as sometimes assumed, that there would be no further changes, but rather that they would all be within the mind-set of liberal democracy, which apparently fulfills mankind's psychological needs. Fukuyama, of course, was writing in the immediate aftermath of the fall of communism and his book bears witness to the widespread complacency of that phase. Since then the dominant mood has altered. The New World Order seems less under control than its proponents imagined. Parts of the globe have been resistant to American political hegemony (and a war on this issue is underway as I write) and the international economic structure has suffered embarrassing instabilities. An influential American statement of this phase is the far less optimistic *The Clash of Civilization and the Remaking of World Order* by Samuel P. Huntington. In Britain recently one of the most publicized accounts of the current situation has been John Gray's *False Dawn: The Delusions of Global Capitalism*. Gray provides a powerful account of the depredations of global capitalism, yet his solution seems too slight. For him capitalism remains but should be controlled and stabilized by better regulation. This is largely a recommendation to carry on as before but within a more safeguarded structure. For Fotopoulos carrying on as before is what got us where we are now. It would involve a failure to learn from previous errors. Only a new structure of life based on different principles would meet the needs of justice and survival. So, where Gray looks for global regulation, Fotopoulos proposes the local community as the prime agency of a renewed and deepened democracy.

For Fotopoulos, as we shall see, a whole change of direction is necessary. Gray's answer, difficult though it might be to achieve, seems unlikely to remedy the condition it describes, particularly as he wants it based on the support of the United States of America. As he tells us: 'A vital condition of reform of the international economy is that it be supported by the world's single most important power. Without active and continuing American endorsement there can be no workable institutions of global governance.'

Fotopoulos, in contrast, doesn't want us to carry on with a modified version of what we had before; indeed, he doesn't think it possible to do so. Fundamental change is necessary, but precisely for that reason it is bound to be much harder to achieve. Fotopoulos could have set himself a more limited, easier and less controversial task; that of delineating our current condition. That would have been a service in itself and the part of the book that deals with it (Part 1) is clear and enlightening. However, our author has a political project, that of fulfilling the democratic ideal that the West nominally professes.

For Fotopoulos 'today's "politics" and "democracy" represent a flagrant distortion of the real meaning of these terms'. He wants a return to the ancient Greek understanding of the concept, which is fair enough in the sense that the word does derive from them, though he does not sufficiently integrate his awareness that the Greeks left out of their democracy those not qualifying for citizenship, 'women, slaves, immigrants'. He takes to task A.H. Birch, the author of a recent textbook on the subject, who, as he realises, is representative of a wide body of current opinion. For most academics in the social sciences, your reviewer included, 'democracy' is regarded as an 'essentially contested concept', whose meaning has altered over time, often according to the wider political purposes being proposed. Greek democracy was a form of rule by the largest class of citizens in a society based on slavery. Since then direct democracy of the citizens has, after a very long interval in which democracy in all its possible forms was totally denigrated, given way to modern representative democracy, with distinct variations between western liberal democracy, third world democracy and even the claims once made by Soviet democracy. The western orthodoxy is that parliamentary liberal democracy is the real thing and that those countries that possess it can enjoy the satisfaction of having fulfilled the democratic ideal. However, Fotopoulos wants a genuine democracy that extends beyond equal voting rights and into the economic sphere. This is a more extended notion of democracy than currently prevails, but one cannot say precisely which definition is right and which is wrong. The contest over the use of political and social words is in itself a political one and so Fotopolous's claim to his sense of the term cannot be accepted as replacing a wrong usage by a right one but merely of stipulating the sense that he will use and the claims that can be made on its behalf. This approach has been strongly challenged in his response to the original version of this review. Fotopoulos asserts that his 'criterion is derived from the Greek etymology of the word' and on that basis concludes 'that any definition that does not involve *direct* self-government of the people is not a proper definition'. He seems to regard all the current understandings of the term as an 'abuse of the word'. On this point I would reply that the English language is full of words whose current meanings have departed from their etymology. Anyone now using current concepts in accord with their supposed original meaning would be incomprehensible to almost everyone else. Consequently, in order to communicate effectively, it is advisable to use words in accord with current usage. Words have their own histories, which are, like all histories, chronologies of change. Here we have a clear clash of approaches, but it is worth stating that this disagreement concerns the philosophy of language rather than the analysis of current politics and society. In conclusion on this issue, I am in full agreement with Fotopoulos when he notes that the contestability of the concept 'is not the real issue. The real issue is which is our primary choice of social paradigm'.

The Rejection of Liberal Democracy

It should be noted that Fotopoulos's definition of democracy is not fully identical with the ancient Greek one. He shares their basic assumption of the 'incompatibility of democracy with any form of concentration of power' and, on that basis, seeks 'a *new* conception of inclusive democracy'. This involves 'the extension of the classical conception of democracy to the social, economic and ecological realms', a demand which, interestingly, had already been made by Pericles. To note that Fotopoulos wants democracy extended should not be taken to imply that he finds it satisfactory in the spheres where it now operates. He seems to have scant regard for liberal democracy. In his 'Response' to me, he declared it 'not difficult to show . . . that liberal democracy does not secure human liberation and it is therefore "wrong"'. This is a rather summary dismissal. I would prefer to say that, as against its predecessors, feudalism and absolute monarchy, liberal democracy represented a major step in a liberatory direction. Indeed, there are vast portions of the globe where it would still do so. This, however, is not Fotopoulos's prime concern. He, rightly, wants to move onward from where we are now.

The core of his rejection of liberal democracy is expressed in his quotation from Bhikhu Parekh:

> Representatives were to be elected by the people, but once elected they were to remain free to manage public affairs as they saw fit. This highly effective way of insulating the government against the full impact of universal franchise lies at the heart of liberal democracy. Strictly speaking liberal democracy is not representative democracy but representative government.

For this reason, even under liberal democracy the political structure is as élite dominated as the economic one. Consequently there is apathy and low turnout, especially among the poor.

In outlining his model of inclusive democracy Fotopoulos combines and builds on the lessons of ancient Greek democracy and the radical critiques of Murray Bookchin and Cornelius Castoriadis. He also works through the radical democratic proposals of Norbert Bobbio, Jürgen Habermas, Chantal Mouffe, Paul Hirst, David Miller and David Held. Fotopolous points out that economic democracy is necessary but not sufficient. Democracy must also extend into the social and the ecological realm; a democracy that centres not so much on the workplace as on the community as a whole. In his plan there are 'no institutionalized political *structures* embodying unequal power relations' for 'the delegation is assigned, on principle, by *lot*, on a rotation basis, and it is always recallable by the citizen body'.

A Libertarian Critique
of Democracy

Michael Munger

Michael Munger is the chair of political science at Duke University. In the following essay, he considers the worth of democracy as a system, examines its flaws, and asks if democracy as it is understood today is a fraud. Munger believes that most Americans simply equate democracy with good governance, which is a complete misunderstanding of the concept, and further that they pay too little attention to what is actually important: the fundamental rights of the people to be free from the tyranny of democracy, or the arbitrary power of government. He says that "democracy" without the safeguards of constitutional liberalism is "both tyrannical and incoherent, the worst system imaginable." According to Munger, collective decision making, in which the majority imposes its rules on the rest, is dangerous, and, the real key to freedom is to liberate people from tyranny by the majority, or freedom from democracy.

Everyone loves democracy. Ask an American if there is a better form of government, and they'll be insulted. You believe in democracy, don't you? And what exactly is it that you believe in? What people mean by "democracy" is some vague combination of good government, protection of individual rights, extremely broad political participation, and widely shared economic prosperity. One might as well throw in an ideal body mass index and a great latke recipe. It's all good, but doesn't mean much, and few people like to think about what democracy really means.

It is fine to celebrate the great achievements of democracies, once they are firmly established. But such celebrations confuse cause and effect. The reason democratic nations have personal liberties, property rights, and rule of law is not that they are democracies. Rather, nations that have those things embody the entire package of the Western tradition of good government. Requiring that government actions hinge on the consent of the governed is the ribbon that holds that bundle together, but it is not the bundle itself. Fareed Zakaria identified this "bundle" problem perfectly.

> For people in the West, democracy means "liberal democracy": a political system marked not only by free and fair elections but also by the rule of law, a separation of powers, and the protection of basic liberties of speech, assembly, religion, and property. *But this bundle of freedoms—what might be termed "constitutional liberalism"—has nothing intrinsically to do with democracy and the two have not always gone together, even in the West.* After all, Adolf Hitler became chancellor of Germany via free elections.

So—just what is democracy? In our mental potpourri, good government leads the list. But then what is 'good government?' A starting point could be voting and majority rule: most people can choose for all of us, and majorities can impose their will on minorities.

Is Democracy a Fraud?

Such blanket endorsements of majority rule make me wonder whether democracy is a fraud or just a conceit. As William Riker pointed out in his 1982 book, *Liberalism Against Populism*, the claim that "fair" processes always, or even often, lead to "good" outcomes ignores much of what is known about institutions and institutional change. If people disagree, and if there are several choices, democracy is manipulable, even dictatorial. For modern political science, this is called the "Arrow Problem," after *Kenneth Arrow*.

If all we mean by democracy is a civil myth, a conceit, it could be useful. The idea of democracy honors common people, calming the mind and pleasing the agora. If democracy is a fraud, however, then we are in bleaker and more sinister terrain. The pretense that in the multitude we find rectitude is dangerous: many of us would love to impose our "wisdom" on others. Saluting the collective wisdom is simply a way to hold other citizens down whilst we steal their purses, or pack their children off to war.

And it has ever been thus. As Polybius tells us:

> The Athenian [democracy] is always in the position of a ship without a commander. In such a ship, if fear of the enemy, or the occurrence of a storm induce the crew to be of one mind and to obey the helmsman, everything goes well; but if they recover from this fear, and begin to treat their officers with contempt, and to quarrel with each other because they are no longer all of one mind,—one party wishing to continue the voyage, and the other urging the steersman to bring the ship to anchor; some letting out the sheets, and others hauling them in, and ordering the sails to be furled,—their discord and quarrels make a sorry show to lookers on; and the position of affairs is full of risk to those on board engaged on the same voyage; and the result has often been that, after escaping the dangers of the widest seas, and the most violent storms, they wreck their ship in harbour and close to shore.

This is not a call for dictatorship, however. The core of the Arrow problem is that societies choose *between* two evils: the tyranny of a Hitler or the potential for incoherence described by Polybius. My thesis is that "democracy" without the safeguards of constitutional liberalism is *both* tyrannical *and* incoherent, the worst system imaginable.

The United States Is Not a Democracy

None of this was news to the American founders. Elections helped citizens control elected officials, and little more. This early skepticism is plain, as in this passage from *Federalist #10*:

A pure democracy, by which I mean a society consisting of a small number of citizens, who assemble and administer the government in person, can admit of no cure for the mischiefs of faction. A common passion or interest will, in almost every case, be felt by a majority of the whole; a communication and concert result from the form of government itself; and there is nothing to check the inducements to sacrifice the weaker party or an obnoxious individual. Hence it is that such democracies have ever been spectacles of turbulence and contention; have ever been found incompatible with personal security or the rights of property; and have in general been as short in their lives as they have been violent in their deaths. Theoretic politicians, who have patronized this species of government, have erroneously supposed that by reducing mankind to a perfect equality in their political rights, they would, at the same time, be perfectly equalized and assimilated in their possessions, their opinions, and their passions.

America is a federal republic, with horizontal separation of powers among executive, legislature, and judiciary, and vertical separation of powers between the central government and the states. The Declaration of Independence is straightforward: the American system is based on the claim that all citizens have rights, and "That to secure these Rights, Governments are instituted among Men, deriving their just Powers from the Consent of the Governed. . . ." That means that elections are still important. We need elections, literally *depend* on them to make the whole system work. But elections are not the ends of government, just the means by which citizens can withhold consent.

The problem is that the rules, procedures, and the basic "machinery" of electoral choice *as a means* have not kept up with the faith people seem to have in democracy *as an end*. We try to divine the will of the people, their "intent" on complex questions. Who can forget Florida in 2000, where officials held ballots over their heads, trying to see light through partially detached bits of cardstock chads?

Elections cannot work this way, not in a nation four time zones wide (not even counting Alaska or Hawaii). Even though in other aspects of our lives we demand instant information, electoral fairness requires that the states withhold information until all the polls are closed. Voting precincts must sacrifice efficiency (which new paperless voting technologies would appear to offer) for legitimacy, where paper receipts are available and where recounts involve actual physical checks of ballots, one by one.

But you knew about this problem, which is mostly technical. I am trying to argue that there is a different problem, at least as important: we *don't just demand too little of our democratic procedures, we are expecting too much of our democratic process*. The educational system in the U.S. has failed students, because we don't know the limits of unlimited democratic choice. We teach that consensus as a value in itself, even though we know that true consensus appears only in dictatorships or narrowly defined decisions. As James Buchanan, Kenneth Arrow, and a host of public choice scholars have shown, *groups cannot be thought to have preferences in the same way that individuals do*. To put it another way, it is perfectly possible, and legitimate, for reasonable people to disagree. The role of democracy is not to banish disagreement, but rather to prevent political disagreements from devolving into armed conflict.

But then in what sense does government depend on "the consent of the governed"? The American system seems cumbersome, but it combines the notion of a republic, where policy choice is indirect, with separation of powers of legislation, where an overlapping consensus is required. A majority of the population is required to pass the House, but a majority in a majority of the states is required to pass the Senate. Then the President, whose constituency is the entire nation, must separately consent before the bill becomes law. The result is far removed from "democracy," but the system does ensure the fundamental democratic principle: government can't do things to us unless we the governed give our consent. Elections are a check on tyranny, not a conjuring of the will of the people.

Where Do We Go from Here?

Policy makers must understand the twin anachronisms that complicate the failures of voting institutions and democratic ideologies in the U.S. There really are two distinct anachronisms, each of which requires immediate attention.

First, our technology of democracy is too old, and prone to abuse or at least distrust. We must bring voting technology into the 21st century, because we accept much less than is possible. We must immediately solve the problem of guaranteeing mechanisms for recording and counting votes that are beyond reproach. As the election of 2004 shows, we are nearly out of time.

Second, our ideology of democracy, our notion of what democracy can accomplish, is anachronistic also. But in this case, the anachronism is not out of the past, but out of a utopian science fiction future. So, we must also take voting ideology *back* to the 19th century, where it belongs. We have come to expect much more than is possible from democracy, and democratic institutions.

This essay may make me sound like an enemy of democracy, some kind of elitist nut. Well, that's not entirely wrong. But describing democracy's flaws is not the same as arguing the virtues of elitism or dictatorship. I just want to foster a humble skepticism about what democracy really is and what it can actually accomplish. Many policy conflicts hinge on whether the public can tell individuals what to do. There is a subtlety that is often missed in policy debate: there is a difference between *public* decisions and *collective* decisions. Public decisions affect everyone by the nature of the choice itself: we can only have one defense budget; polluting rivers befouls not just my water, but yours.

Collective decisions, on the other hand, affect us all only because the majority is empowered to force its will on everyone. There need be no true public aspects to the decision as a policy outcome; we have just chosen to take the decision out of individuals' hands and put the power in the hands of the mob.

Now, it may very well be the case that lots of collective decisions are also public. But we need to see the line dividing private and collective choices, and to defend it fiercely. As P. J. O'Rourke notes, the fact that a majority likes something doesn't mean that the majority should get to choose that something for everyone.

> Now, majority rule is a precious, sacred thing worth dying for. But—like other precious, sacred things, such as the home and the family—it's not only worth dying for; it can make you wish you were dead. Imagine if all of life were determined by majority rule. Every meal would be a pizza. Every pair of pants, even those in a Brooks Brothers suit, would be stone-washed denim. Celebrity diets and exercise books would be the only thing on the shelves at the library. And—since women are a majority of the population, we'd all be married to Mel Gibson.

The real key to freedom is to secure people from tyranny by the majority, or freedom *from* democracy. The problem, then, is what Fareed Zakaria has called "illiberal democracy." The metaphor we use to understand ourselves matters, because it figures in how we try to advise others.

> For much of modern history, what characterized governments in Europe and North America, and differentiated them from those around the world, was not democracy but

constitutional liberalism. The "Western model of government" is best symbolized not by the mass plebiscite but the impartial judge.

The framers of the U.S. Constitution fully recognized that there is nothing, nothing at all, inherent in democracy that ensures the freedom of persons or property. When we advise other nations about how to devise better systems of government, our own historical skepticism about the power of pure democracy can be neglected only at our peril. When we help a developing nation design its government, we need unashamedly to advocate something like the U.S. model. Thomas Hobbes said "Covenants, without the Sword, are but words." The modern equivalent might be this: "Democracy, without the Bill of Rights, is but tyranny."

Some Aspects of the U.S. Electoral System Hinder True Democracy

Lani Guinier

Lani Guinier is a professor at Harvard Law School who spent many years working on civil rights issues for the National Association for the Advancement of Colored People and in the U.S. Justice Department under President Carter. In the following piece, Guinier discusses how the 2000 presidential election highlighted flaws in the U.S. electoral system that make it less than truly democratic. While under the law every person's vote should count equally, Guinier argues that in practice the system places many obstacles in the way of poor and minority voters. Furthermore, she believes it is inherently unfair to give the winner of an election, by no matter how small a margin, all of the power. Better, Guinier believes, is proportional democracy as practiced in Europe and elsewhere. In that system, even those whose political opinions are in the minority can still gain significant representation in government.

For years many of us have been calling for a national conversation about what it means to be a multiracial democracy. We have enumerated the glaring flaws inherent in our winner-take-all form of voting, which has produced a steady decline in voter participation, underrepresentation of women and racial minorities in office, lack of meaningful competition and choice in most elections, and the general failure of politics to mobilize, inform, and inspire half the eligible electorate. Still, nothing changed. Democracy was an asterisk in political debate and the diagnosis for what ailed it was encompassed in vague references to "campaign finance reform." But the harm was not just in the money and its sources; the problem has been the rules of American democracy itself.

Enter Florida and the surprising intervention by the United States Supreme Court in *Bush v. Gore*. On December 12, 2000, the Supreme Court selected the next president when, in the name of George W. Bush's rights to equal protection of the laws, it stopped the recounting of votes. Excoriated at the time for deciding an election, the Court majority's stout reading of equal protection is an invitation not just to future litigation but to a citizens' movement for genuine participatory democracy. The Court's decision—and the colossal legal fight that preceded it—might stimulate a real national debate about democracy. At minimum the ruling calls on us to consider what it means to be a multiracial democracy that has equal protection as its first principle.

The decision invites future litigants to rely on the Court's newfound equal protection commitments to enforce uniform standards for casting and tabulating votes in federal elections from state to state, county to county, and within counties. The conservative majority found that the source of the fundamental nature of the right to vote "lies in the equal weight accorded to each vote and the equal dignity owed to each voter." We have not heard such a full-throated representation of the equal protection clause in many years, at least not with regard to the rights of voters to do more than cast a ballot. This language harkens back to the broad commitment we once heard from the 1960s-era Warren Court, which affirmed the people's fundamental right to exercise their suffrage "in a free and unimpaired manner." Concerned that the lack of uniform standards for a manual recount would lead to "arbitrary and disparate treatment" of the members of the Florida electorate, the majority relied on two expansive Supreme Court decisions. *Harper v. Virginia Board of Elections* and *Reynolds v. Sims*. These cases, from the salad days of the Warren Court, explicitly affirm Lincoln's vision of government of the people, by the people, for the people. Perhaps—in the name of restoring "voter confidence in the outcome of elections"—the conservative majority will now welcome, as it did in *Bush v. Gore*, other lawsuits that seek to challenge the very discretion the five-vote majority found so troublesome when exercised by local Florida county officials. Perhaps not.

It seems unlikely, of course, that the conservative majority will act in the future to rehabilitate our partial democracy. Some commentators undoubtedly will argue that the *per curiam* decision only addresses the remedial power of a state court seeking a statewide remedy. Others will point to the great irony that the Court has shown itself more deeply committed to safeguarding the rights of a major-party candidate than to protecting disenfranchised voters across the board.

The *Bush v. Gore* majority, which went out on a limb to protect the rights of a single litigant, George W. Bush, has been noticeably less exercised about arbitrary or disparate treatment when such considerations are raised by voters who are racial minorities. Indeed, in a 1994 concurring opinion, when the claim to a meaningful and equally valued vote was raised by black litigants, Justice Clarence Thomas declared that the Court should avoid examining "electoral mechanisms that may affect the 'weight' given to a ballot duly cast." Even where congressional statutes, such as the Voting Rights Act, explicitly define the term "voting" to "include all action necessary to make a vote effective," Justice Thomas urged the Court to ignore the actual text of the statute.

The *Bush v. Gore* invitation to value votes equally, in order to "sustain the confidence that all citizens must have in the outcome of elections," should be heeded, but not in the form of legal wrangling before a judge. That it is time for political agitation rather than judicial activism may be the most important contribution of the *Bush v. Gore* opinion. In fact, that is already happening, at least in the law schools. The *New York*

Times reported on February 1, 2001—almost three months after the election—that the decision continues to generate a beehive of activity among law professors furious at the Supreme Court's role. The debate in law schools already has the "flavor of the teachins of the Vietnam War era, when professors spurred their students to political action." As during the movements for abolition, women's suffrage, and black voting rights, we, the people, must take up the burden.

Indeed, the Court's choice of language explicitly valuing "no person's vote over another's" ought to launch a citizens' movement similar to the 1960s civil rights marches that led to the Voting Rights Act, demonstrations in which citizens carried banners with the "one person, one vote" slogan. One vote, one value—meaning that everyone's vote should count toward the election of someone he or she voted for—should be the rallying cry of all who wish to restore the confidence that even the conservative Court majority agrees "all citizens must have in the outcome of elections." This movement, let's recall, began in the streets, was cautiously then boldly embraced by liberal politicians, and eventually led to raised grassroots consciousness as well as national legislation. That is how democratic movements change the course of events—and in the process enrich and renew democracy.

Where Is the Outrage?

Certainly many people outside the legal academy continue to feel alienated by the outcome of this presidential election. A survey released in early December from the Harvard Vanishing Voter project suggests that large majorities of the American people believe election procedures have been "unfair to the voters." Not surprisingly, nationwide those most likely to feel disenfranchised are blacks. In December 2000, almost 90 percent of black voters felt that way. One out of 10 blacks reported that they or someone in their family had trouble voting, according to a national report produced by Michael Dawson and Lawrence Bobo, of the Center for the Study of Race, Politics and Culture, and the W.E.B. Du Bois Institute. A CBS News poll, made public on the eve of the inauguration, found that 51 percent of the respondents said they considered Bush's victory a legitimate one, but only 19 percent of Democrats and 12 percent of blacks said so.

The anger over what happened in Florida has only been reinforced by the failure of the Democratic Party leadership to move quickly and seriously to engage the legitimacy issue. Right after November 7, when the perception first emerged that the election was being hijacked, the Gore campaign actively discouraged mass protest. On January 12, when Al Gore presided over the counting of the electoral college votes, it was only members of the Congressional Black Caucus (CBC) who rose, one by one, to protest the filing of Florida's votes. They could not get a single Democratic senator (from a body that includes not a single black representative) to join their objection. The silence of the white Democrats in Congress turned the CBC demonstration into an emphatic recapitulation of the election drama. As the presiding officer, Al Gore overruled the protests. The moment was especially poignant, because the Black Caucus members, in speaking out for Floridians whose votes were not counted, were speaking out for all Americans, while even their progressive white colleagues sat in awkward silence. E.J. Dionne, a columnist for *The Washington Post*, watched the drama unfold on television. Turning to his eight-year-old son, seated next to him, Dionne explained, "They are speaking out for us too."

"It was the Black Caucus, and the Black Caucus alone," James Carroll wrote in *The Boston Globe* "that showed itself sensitive to . . . what is clearly true about the recent presidential election in Florida." That truth is the gap between what the rules permit and what democracy requires. Florida made it obvious that our winner-take-all rules would unfairly award all of Florida's electoral college votes to one candidate even though the margin of victory was less than the margin of error. Yet our elected officials in Washington are committed to those rules and, even more, to maintaining civility between those adversely affected by the rules and those who benefited. As Carroll wrote, "Those who sit atop the social and economic pyramid always speak of love, while those at the bottom always speak of justice."

The CBC protest shows that outrage over the election continues. But the CBC protest also speaks to the fact that the conversation about the true meaning of democracy is not happening yet, at least not at the highest levels of government. There is talk, of course, about fixing the mechanics of election balloting; but it is the rules themselves, and not just the vote-counting process, that are broken. This is all the more reason that the conversation, which needs to address issues of justice, not just compassion, also needs to rise up from communities as a citizens' movement.

Those who were disenfranchised—disproportionately black, poorer, and less well educated—were not asking for pity; they wanted democracy. Stories of long lines at polling places, confusing ballots, and strict limitations on how long voters could spend in the voting booth help explain why turnout numbers are skewed toward those who are wealthy, white, and better educated. We are a democracy that supposedly believes in universal suffrage, and yet the different turnout rates between high-income and low-income voters are far greater than in Europe, where they range from 5 percent to 10 percent. More than two-thirds of people in America with incomes greater than $50,000 voted, compared with one-third of those with incomes under $10,000. Many poor people are also less literate; for them time limits and complex ballots proved disabling when the menu of candidates was organized around lists of individuals rather than easily identified icons for political parties. Indeed, more ballots were "spoiled" in the presidential race than were cast for so-called spoiler Ralph Nader.

The shocking number of invalid ballots is a direct result of antiquated voting mechanics, an elitist view of the relationship between education and citizenship, and an individualistic view of political participation that would shame any nation that truly believes in broad citizen participation.

Class, Race And Balloting

In addition to class, the window into the workings of Florida's balloting allowed us to see how race affects—and in turn is affected by—voting rules and procedures. The election debacle revealed gaps not just in our democracy but in the way our democracy racializes public policy and then disenfranchises the victims of those policies. Old voting machines, more likely to reject ballots not perfectly completed, were disproportionately located in low-income and minority neighborhoods. These problems contributed to stunning vote-rejection numbers. According to *The New York Times* black precincts in Miami-Dade County had votes thrown out at twice the rate of Hispanic (primarily Cuban and Republican) precincts and at close to four times the rate of white precincts. In that county alone, in predominantly black precincts, the *Times* said, "one in 11 ballots were rejected, . . . a total at 9,904"—thousands more than Bush's margin of victory. The balloting rules in Florida did not just incidentally disenfranchise minority voters; they apparently resulted from what many think were aggressive efforts to suppress black turnout. The *New York Times* also reported that county officials in Miami-Dade gave certain precincts—mostly the Hispanic (that is, Cuban and Republican) ones—laptop computers so that they could check names against the central county voter file. In black precincts, where there were a lot of recently registered voters whose names didn't appear on the local list, the precinct workers were not given computers and were supposed to call the county office to check the list—but no one answered the phones or the lines were busy, so countless voters, who were in fact registered, were just sent away.

Florida's minority residents and many others faced another structural hurdle to having their voices heard. Anyone convicted of a felony is permanently banned from voting in Florida and 12 other states (disproportionately from the old Confederacy) even after they have paid their debt to society. As a result, 13 percent of black men nationwide and in some southern states as many as 30 percent of black men are disenfranchised. In Florida alone, more than 400,000 ex-felons, almost half of them black, could not vote last November. Also worth noting is that before the election Florida's secretary of state hired a firm to conduct a vigorous cleansing of the voting rolls—not just of Florida's felons, but also of ex-offenders from other states whose rights had been restored in those states and who were thus still legally eligible to vote in Florida. The Hillsborough County elections supervisor, for example, found that 54 percent of the voters targeted by the "scrub" were black, in a county where blacks make up 11 percent of the voting population. While Canada takes special steps to register former prisoners and encourage citizenship, Florida and other states ostracize them.

One short-term solution to the problem of the disenfranchised ex-offender population is to lobby state legislators to abolish the permanent disenfranchisement of felons. Alternatively, Congress could pass a statute providing voting rights for all ex-felons in federal elections.

The Soul of a Democracy Movement

Unfortunately, in pursuit of bipartisan civility, the Democratic Party leadership appears to be marching to a false harmony: Charmed by compassionate conservatism and conscious of middle-of-the-road swing voters' aversion to conflict, top Democrats have ignored issues of justice and the troubling disenfranchisement of many of the party's most loyal supporters. If we learn anything from the Supreme Court's role in the

2000 election travesty, it must be that when the issue is justice, the people—not the justices of the Court or the Democratic leaders in Washington—will lead. And if anything is true about the fiasco in Florida, it is the need for new leaders who are willing to challenge rather than acquiesce to unfair rules. New leadership will not come from a single, charismatic figure orchestrating deals out of Washington, D.C.; nor will it be provided by a group devoted only to remedying the disenfranchisement of black voters. What is needed instead is a courageous assembly of stalwart individuals who are willing to ask the basic questions the Black Caucus members raised—questions that go to the very legitimacy of our democratic procedures, not just in Florida but nationwide. These are likely to be individuals organized at the local level, possibly even into a new political party that is broadly conceived and dedicated to real, participatory democracy. Such a movement could build on the energy of black voter participation, which between 1996 and last year went from 10 percent to 15 percent in Florida and from 5 percent to 12 percent in Missouri.

But while black anger could fuel a citizens' movement or a new, European-style political party that seeks reforms beyond the mechanics of election day voting, the danger is that whites will be suspicious of the struggle if they perceive that its aim is simply to redress wrongs done to identifiable victims or to serve only the interests of people of color. And people of color can alienate potential supporters if they focus exclusively on vindicating the rights of minority voters and fail to emphasize three dramatic distortions in our present rules that undermine the ability of low-income and working people, women, and progressives, as well as racial minorities, to participate in a genuinely democratic transformation. These rules (1) limit voting to 12 hours on a workday and require registration weeks or even months in advance; (2) disenfranchise prisoners for the purpose of voting but count them for the purpose of allocating legislative seats, and (3) waste votes through winner-take-all elections. A pro-democracy movement has a good chance to succeed if it focuses on unfair rules whose dislocations may be felt first by blacks but whose effects actually disempower vast numbers of people across the country.

A pro-democracy movement would need to build on the experience of Florida to show how problems with disenfranchisement based on race and status signify systemic issues of citizen participation. Such mobilization would seek to recapture the passion in evidence immediately after the election as union leaders, civil rights activists, black elected officials, ministers, rabbis, and the president of the Haitian women's organization came together at a black church in Miami, reminded the assembly of the price their communities had paid for the right to vote, and vowed never to be disfranchised again. "It felt like Birmingham last night," Mari Castellanos, a Latina activist in Miami, wrote in an e-mail describing the mammoth rally at the 14,000-member New Birth Baptist Church, a primarily African-American congregation.

> The sanctuary was standing room only. So were the overflow rooms and the school hall, where congregants connected via large TV screens. . . . The people sang and prayed and listened. Story after story was told of voters being turned away at the polls, of ballots being allegedly destroyed, of NAACP election literature being allegedly discarded at the main post office, of Spanish-speaking poll workers being sent to Creole precincts and vice-versa.

Although not encouraged by Democratic Party leaders, by joining their voices these Florida voters were beginning to realize their collective potential—as ordinary citizens—to become genuine democrats (with a small d). By highlighting our nation's wretched record on voting rules and practices, these impassioned citizens were raising the obvious questions: Do those in charge really want large citizen participation, especially if that means more participation by poor people and people of color? Even more, do Americans of all incomes and races realize that everyone loses when we tolerate disenfranchisement of some? And how can we tolerate the logjam of winner-take-all two-party monopoly, especially at the local level?

Enriching Democratic Choice

As the Florida meltdown suggests, the problem includes mechanical defects, but it is the rules themselves, not just old technology, that limit the political clout of entire communities. Weak democracy feeds on itself. There are some technical fixes worth pursuing [see "Reclaiming Democracy" by Burt Neuborne, and "Democracy's Moment" by Miles Rapoport]. But reform of voting mechanisms—while important—is not enough. The circumstances of this last election call for a larger focus on issues of representation and participation. A longer-term and more-far-ranging solution to the problems in Florida as well as those around the country would be to enrich democracy by broadening ways of reflecting and encouraging voter preferences.

For example, in South Africa, where the black majority now shares political power with the white minority, there is a successful system of proportional representation. Voters cast their ballots for the political party they feel most represents their interests, and the party gets seats in the legislature in proportion to the number of votes it receives. Instead of a winner-take-all situation in which there are losers who feel completely unrepresented when their candidate doesn't capture the top number of votes, each vote counts to enhance the political power of the party of the voters' choice. Under South Africa's party-list system, the party that gets 30 percent of the vote gets 30 percent of the seats. Or if the party gets only 10 percent of the vote, it still gets 10 percent of the seats in the legislature. Only because of this system does South Africa's white minority have any representation in the national legislature. Ironically, South Africa, only seven years out of apartheid, is more advanced in terms of practicing democratic principles than the United States is 150 years after slavery and 40 years after Jim Crow.

As June Zeitlin, executive director of the Women's Environment and Development Organization points out, proportional representation systems also benefit women. In a letter that The New York Times declined to publish, Zeitlin wrote: "Women are grossly underrepresented at all levels of government worldwide. However, women fare significantly better in proportional representation electoral systems. . . . The 10 countries with the highest percentage of women in parliament have systems that include proportional representation." Zeitlin, who spearheads a campaign—50/50 Get the Balance Right—aimed at increasing women's participation in government, has noticed that proportional representation mechanisms work in many countries in tandem with the deliberate political goals of progressive parties.

Proportional representation reforms for legislative bodies, even Congress, would not even require an amendment to the U.S. Constitution. Nothing in the Constitution says that we have to use winner-take-all single-member districts. Since seizing the initiative in 1995, two Democratic members of the Congressional Black Caucus, Representatives Cynthia McKinney of Georgia and Mel Watt of North Carolina, have repeatedly introduced legislation called the Voter Choice Act, which provides for states to choose proportional representation voting. It's a system that should have great appeal not just for African Americans but for every group that has ever felt disenfranchised.

A pro-democracy movement would look seriously at forms of proportional representation that could assure Democrats in Florida, Republicans in Democratic-controlled states, and racial minorities and women in all states fair representation in the state legislatures. It would focus renewed attention on the importance of minority voters—racial, political, and urban minorities—gaining a more meaningful voice as well as a real opportunity to participate throughout the democratic process and not just on election day.

Chronology

2500 and 4000 BCE

Sumerian city-states of Mesopotamia (modern-day Iraq) are believed to have developed some form of democratic governance.

600 BCE **to** AD **200**

Sovereign republics are thought to have existed in parts of India.

Late 500s BCE

The lawmaker and statesman Solon initiates economic, social reforms, and constitutional reforms in Athens.

509 BCE **to 31** BCE

Romans construct a new form of political organization—the republic.

508 BCE

The aristocrat Cleisthenes gains political power in Athens.

505 to 502 BCE

Cleisthenes introduces a series of political reforms leading to the formation of Athenian democracy.

460 to 429 BCE

The general Pericles controls Athenian affairs, radicalizing Athenian democracy.

338 BCE

Philip of Macedon conquers Athens, signaling the end of Athenian democracy.

27 BCE

The Gaius Julius Caesar Octavianus is awarded title of Augustus by a decree of the Senate, making him emperor of Rome and bringing to an end the Roman republic.

1000 to 1450

The Iroquois and other indigenous peoples of the Americas are said to begun to practice the type of democracy found in the United States Constitution through self-governing territories that were part of a larger whole.

1215

King John of England signs the Magna Carta, the "Great Charter," creating the English "Parliament" and stating that written laws hold a higher power than the king, limiting the power of the monarch and giving some power to the people.

1265

In England, Simon de Montfort introduces the idea that power-holders are responsible to an electorate and calls the first directly-elected parliament in medieval Europe.

Late 13th century to 18th century

Republican city states, including Venice and Florence, flourish in Italy.

1500s

The Nobles' Commonwealth, in which aristocrats freely elect their monarch, exists in Poland.

1628

In England, the Petition of Right stipulates that the monarch can no longer tax without parliament's permission.

1642-1651

The English Civil War is fought between monarchists and parliamentarians, which ends with the establishment of the English Commonwealth.

1660

The monarchy is restored in England.

1689

The English Bill of Rights provides freedom of speech for citizens and bans cruel or unusual punishment.

1690

John Locke publishes *Two Treatises of Government.*

1755

The Corsican republic is established, which adopts a constitution based on enlightenment principles and implements women's suffrage.

1762

Jean Jacques Rousseau publishes *The Social Contract.*

1775 to 1783

The American War of Independence is fought by the Revolutionaries in the American colonies against the British government.

1776

The Declaration of Independence is signed.

1787

The United States constitution is adopted. It is ratified in 1789.

1789 to 1799

The French governmental structure undergoes radical change during the French Revolution. Revolutionary France adopts the *Declaration of the Rights of Man and of the Citizen.*

1791

The Haitian Revolution establishes a free republic.

1848

The National Woman Suffrage Association is formed in the United States.

1850s

The secret ballot is introduced in Australia; it is adopted in 1892 in the United States.

1863

In the United States, the Emancipation Proclamation promises freedom to slaves in the American Confederacy.

1906

Full modern democratic rights and universal suffrage for all citizens are implemented constitutionally in Finland.

1918

Universal suffrage is achieved in Britain.

1920

In the United States, women are granted the right to vote.

1947

Japan adopts a democratic constitution.

1950

India becomes a democratic republic upon achieving independence from Great Britain. In the next decade, a number of former British colonies achieve independence and adopt democratic forms of government.

1965

The Voting Rights Act in the United States protects every American against racial discrimination in voting.

1974

30 countries in the world are considered democratic.

1970s and 1980s

New waves of democracy sweep across Southern Europe and Central Europe.

1990s and 2000s

Countries in Eastern Europe, Latin America, Asia, Africa, and the Middle East move towards greater democracy.

2008

117 of the world's 192 countries are considered democratic.

Organizations to Contact

The editors have compiled the following list of organizations concerned with the issues debated in this book. The descriptions are derived from materials provided by the organizations. All have publications or information available for interested readers. The list was compiled on the date of publication of the present volume; the information provided here may change. Readers need to remember that many organizations take several weeks or longer to respond to inquiries.

Amnesty International
1 Easton St., London WC1X 0DW UK
www.amnesty.org

Amnesty International is a worldwide movement of people who campaign for internationally recognized human rights for all. Its supporters work to improve human rights through campaigning and international solidarity. The organization has more than 2.2 million members and subscribers in more than 150 countries and regions who coordinate this support to act for justice on a wide range of issues, including civil and political rights.

Center for Civic Participation (CCP)
1313 SE 5th St., Ste. 113, Minneapolis, MN 55414
(612) 331-7440 • fax: (612) 331-7447
www.centerforcivicparticipation.org

The CCP's mission is to increase civic engagement by individuals and organizations in ways that both strengthen American democratic institutions and encourage public involvement in civic life. CCP's priority is to work in communities that have been historically underrepresented in the democratic process.

Center for the Evolution of Democracy (CED)
PO Box 1329, Martinez, CA   94553-7329
fax: (510) 845-7847

The CED is a nonprofit, public benefit corporation founded in 1994 to promote a deeper understanding of democracy as a decision-making process. The organization bases its work on the idea that democracy as it exists today, is only a partial implementation of an ancient idea that still has profound implications for the evolution of human life. It seeks to explore new conceptualizations of democracy within the modern and postmodern context and reform the world's democracies.

Center for Media and Democracy
520 University Ave., Ste. 227, Madison, WI   53703
(608) 260-9713 • fax: (608) 260-9714
www.prwatch.org

The Center for Media and Democracy is a nonprofit, nonpartisan, public interest organization that strengthens participatory democracy by investigating and exposing public relations spin and propaganda, and by promoting media literacy and citizen journalism.

Civil Society International (CSI)
2929 NE Blakeley St., Seattle, WA   98105
(206) 523-4755
www.civilsoc.org

CSI assists independent organizations working for democracy and civil society in countries closed, or inhospitable, to these principles. The group brings together in one place information about projects worldwide committed to the keystones of civil society: limited government, popular elections, and the rule of law; free association and expression; regulated, but open and market-oriented economies; aid to the poor, orphaned, elderly, sick, or disabled; and finally, civic cultures that value pluralism and individual liberty but also respect human needs for community and shared visions of the common good.

Freedom House
Freedom House, Washington, DC   20036
www.freedomhouse.org

Freedom House, founded in 1941 by Eleanor Roosevelt, Wendell Willkie, and other Americans concerned with the mounting threats to peace and democracy, is a nonprofit, nonpartisan organization that advocates for democracy and freedom around the world. Through a vast array of international programs and publications, Freedom House is working to advance the worldwide expansion of political and economic freedom. *Freedom in the World*, Freedom House's flagship publication, is a comparative assessment of global political rights and civil liberties. Published annually since 1972, the survey ratings and narrative reports on 193 countries and 15 related and disputed territories are used by policy makers, the media, international corporations, civic activists, and human rights defenders to monitor trends in democracy and track improvements and setbacks in freedom worldwide.

IFES
1101 15th St. NW, Third Floor, Washington, DC   20005
(202) 350-6700 • fax: (202) 452-0804
www.ifes.org

IFES is a nonprofit democracy development organization that works to give people a voice in the way that they are governed. Formerly the International Foundation for Election Systems, IFES is the world's premiere election assistance organization, providing countries with the technical advice and tools they need to run democratic elections.

International Endowment for Democracy (IED)
4 Washington Square Village, Apt. 9A, New York, NY   10012
www.iefd.org

IED is a foundation of progressive American scholars, lawyers and activists dedicated to promoting democracy in the United States, The organization supports progressive workers' groups,

221

progressive media, progressive education, and investigations into the undemocratic practices of the United States while it engages in promoting "democratic nation building" in other countries.

International Institute for Democracy and Electoral Assistance (International IDEA)

Strömsborg, Stockholm   SE-103 34
  Sweden
+46 8 698 37 00 • fax: +46 8 20 24 22
www.idea.int

International IDEA is an intergovernmental organization that supports sustainable democracy worldwide. Its objective is to strengthen democratic institutions and processes. International IDEA acts as a catalyst for democracy building by providing knowledge resources, expertise, and a platform for debate on democracy issues. It works together with policy makers, donor governments, United Nations organizations and agencies, regional organizations and others engaged in democracy building.

National Endowment for Democracy (NED)

1025 F St. NW, Ste. 800, Washington, DC   20004
(202) 378-9700
www.ned.org

The NED is a private, nonprofit organization created in 1983 that seeks to strengthen democratic institutions around the world through nongovernmental efforts. The endowment is governed by an independent, nonpartisan board of directors, but it promotes a clearly conservative political agenda. With its annual congressional appropriation, it makes hundreds of grants each year to support groups in Africa, Asia, Central and Eastern Europe, Latin America, the Middle East, and the former Soviet Union. Staff members are available to comment on democratic development and related topics in Africa, Asia, Central Europe, Eurasia, Latin America, and the Middle East.

World Movement for Democracy
1025 F St. NW, Washington, DC   20004
(202) 378-9700
www.wmd.org

The World Movement for Democracy is an international network of organizations that share a common goal of promoting democracy. Its mission is "to strengthen democracy where it is weak, to reform and invigorate democracy even where it is long-standing, and to bolster pro-democracy groups in countries that have not yet entered into a process of democratic transition." It was initiated in 1999 by the National Endowment for Democracy and two Indian nongovernmental organizations.

World Youth Movement for Democracy (WYMD)
www.ymd.youthlink.org/ymd/index.html

The WYMD, founded in 2004, aims to serve as a platform for young activists to address the importance of promoting democratic values, a forum for sharing information and ideas, and an action-oriented, solidarity movement. It provides a space for young activists to build relationships with each other, to collaborate across borders, to deepen their knowledge on key issues, and to develop practical skills. The World Youth Movement aims to support youth participation in efforts to strengthen democracy where it is weak, to reform and invigorate democracy even where it is long-standing, and to bolster pro-democracy groups in countries that have not yet entered into a process of democratic transition.

Bibliography

Books

Aristotle   *The Politics*. Sioux Falls, SD: NuVision, 2004.

Benjamin Barber   *Strong Democracy*. Los Angeles: University of California Press, 1984.

Andrew Carnegie   *Triumphant Democracy*. Boston: Adamant Media, 2002.

Noam Chomsky   Deterring Democracy. New York: Hill & Wang, 1992.

Robert A. Dahl   *Democracy and Its Critics*. New Haven, CT: Yale University Press, 1991.

Robert A. Dahl   *On Democracy*. New Haven, CT: Yale University Press, 1999.

John Dewey   *Democracy and Education*. New York: Macmillan, 1923.

Cynthia Farrar   *The Origins of Democratic Thinking: The Invention of Politics in Classical Athens*. Cambridge, UK: Cambridge University Press, 1988.

Francis Fukuyama   *The End of History and the Last Man*. Harmondsworth, UK: Penguin, 1992.

Al Gore   *The Assault on Reason*. New York: Penguin, 2007.

Alexander Hamilton, John Jay, and James Madison	*The Federalist Papers*. New York: Penguin, 1987.
David Held	"Democracy and Globalization." In *Re-Imagining Political Community: Studies in Cosmopolitan Democracy*. Eds. Daniele Archibugi, David Held, and Martin Köhler. Stanford, CA: Stanford University Press, 1998.
Thomas Hobbes	*Leviathan*. New York: Touchstone, 1997.
Thomas Jefferson	*Political Writings*. Eds. Joyce Oldham Appleby and Terrence Bal. Cambridge, UK: Cambridge University Press, 1996.
Michael Mandelbaum	*Democracy's Good Name: The Rise and Risks of the World's Most Popular Form of Government*. New York: Public Affairs, 2007.
Masaso Maruyama	Thought and Behavior in Modern Japanese Politics. Ed. Ivan Morris. Oxford, UK: Oxford University Press, 1963.
Andrew McGrew, ed.	*The Transformation of Democracy?* Cambridge, UK: Polity, 1997.
John Rawls	*A Theory of Justice*. Oxford, UK: Clarendon Press, 1972.
Amartya Sen	*Identity and Violence: The Illusion of Destiny*. New York: W.W. Norton, 2007.

Vandana Shiva	*Earth Democracy: Justice, Sustainability, and Peace*. Boston: South End, 2005.
Adam Smith	*The Wealth of Nations*. New York: Bantam Classics, 2003.
Charles Tilly	*Democracy* Cambridge, UK: Cambridge University Press, 2007.
H.G. Wells	*The Future in America*. New York: Harper, 1906.

Periodicals

Amr Hamzawy	"Liberty and Justice for Some." *Economist.com*, August 22, 2007.
	"Is the U.S. Through with Arab Democracy?" *Mother Jones*, June 26, 2006.
Naomi Klein	"Big Brother Democracy." *The Nation*, August 23, 2007.
Paul Skidmore	"Disenchanted Democracies." *Prospect Magazine*, February 2008.
Graham Usher	"Trappings of Democracy in Pakistan." *The Nation*, November 15, 2007.
Walter Williams	"Do We Want Democracy?" *Capitalism Magazine*, June 22, 2002.
Fareed Zakaria	"Elections Are Not Democracy." *Newsweek*, February 2005

Index